Practical Exercises for ECDL Expert Using Office XP

PEARSON
Education

We work with the leading authors to develop the
strongest educational materials in computing, bringing
cutting-edge thinking and best learning practice to a
global market.

Under a range of well-known imprints, including
Prentice Hall we craft high quality print and electronic
publications which help readers to understand and
apply their content, whether studying or at work.

To find out more about the complete range of our
publishing, please visit us on the World Wide Web at:
www.pearsoned.co.uk

Jackie Sherman

Practical Exercises for ECDL Expert Using Office XP

Prentice
Hall

An imprint of **Pearson Education**

London · Boston · Indianapolis · New York · Mexico City · Toronto · Sydney · Tokyo
Singapore · Hong Kong · Cape Town · Madrid · Paris · Amsterdam · Munich · Milan

Pearson Education Limited
Edinburgh Gate
Harlow
Essex CM2O 2JE
England

and Associated Companies throughout the world

Visit us on the World Wide Web at:
www.pearsoned.co.uk

First published 2007

The questions and exercises found in this book have been written especially for it. You can
find official sample questions on the ECDL website: www.ecdl.com

All product and company names are ™ or ® trademarks of their respective owners. Pearson
Education Limited has made every effort to seek permission to use the screenshots used in
this book.

Microsoft product screen shots reprinted with permission from Microsoft Corporation.

European Computer Driving Licence, ECDL, International Computer Driving Licence, ICDL, e-Citizen
and related logos are trade marks of The European Computer Driving Licence Foundation Limited
("ECDL-F") in Ireland and other countries.

Pearson Education Ltd is an entity independent of ECDL-F and is not associated with ECDL-F in any
manner. This courseware publication may be used to assist candidates to prepare for the ECDL
examination. Neither ECDL-F nor Pearson Education Ltd warrants that the use of this courseware
publication will ensure passing of the ECDL examination. This courseware publication has been
independently reviewed and approved by ECDL-F as complying with the following standard:

> *Technical compliance with the learning objectives ECDL Syllabus Version 4.0.*

Confirmation of this approval can be obtained by reviewing the Courseware Section of the website
www.ecdl.com

The material contained in this courseware publication has not been reviewed for technical accuracy and
does not guarantee that candidates will pass [insert name of relevant test(s)]. Any and all assessment items
and/or performance-based exercises contained in this courseware publication relate solely to this
publication and do not constitute or imply certification by ECDL-F in respect of the ECDL examination or
any other ECDL-F test.

Irrespective of how the material contained in this courseware is deployed, for example in a learning
management system (LMS) or a customized interface, nothing should suggest to the candidate that this
material constitutes certification or can lead to certification through any other process than official
ECDL/ICDL certification testing.

For details on sitting the ECDL examination and other ECDL-F tests in your country, please contact your
country's National ECDL/ICDL designated Licensee or visit ECDL-F's web site at www.ecdl.com.

Candidates using this courseware publication must be registered with the National Licensee, before
undertaking the ECDL examination. Without a valid registration, the ECDL examination cannot be
undertaken and no ECDL certificate, nor any other form of recognition, can be given to a candidate.

Registration should be undertaken with your country's National ECDL/ICDL designated Licensee at any
Approved ECDL Test Centre.

ECDL Syllabus 4.0 is the official syllabus of the ECDL certification programme at the date of approval of
this courseware publication.

ISBN-13: 978-0-13-174393-9
ISBN-10: 0-13-174393-7

British Library Cataloguing-in-Publication Data
A catalogue record for this book is available from the British Library

Library of Congress Cataloging-in-Publication Data
A catalogue record for this book is available from the British Library

10 9 8 7 6 5 4 3 2 1
11 10 09 08 07 06

Typeset in 10/13 pt Stone Serif by 30
Printed and bound by Bell & Bain Ltd, Glasgow

The publisher's policy is to use paper manufactured from sustainable forests.

Contents

Introduction

Many people now take the ECDL: a seven module IT qualification covering all the basic skills needed to work effectively on a computer. It includes using e-mail, searching the Internet, word processing and creating spreadsheets, charts, databases and presentations.

If you want more of a challenge, you need to take ECDL Advanced. This is a four module qualification covering advanced features of four major applications: word processing, spreadsheets and charts, databases and presentation software.

To pass each of the ECDL Advanced modules, you must take a one hour paper consisting of 20 questions.

Although there is no requirement to have passed ECDL before attempting the Advanced syllabus, knowledge of computer applications at this more basic level will be assumed. If you do not have the qualification, you may like to look at *Practical Exercises for ECDL* to check that you have the necessary skills.

The ECDL Advanced modules can be taken individually, but if you pass all four you can achieve the status of an ECDL Expert with its associated benefits. Full details of the ECDL Advanced syllabus, test centres and how to become an ECDL Expert can be found at www.ecdl.co.uk and www.ecdlexpert.co.uk.

Practical Exercises for ECDL Expert Using Office XP has been written to give you the necessary practice in order to pass the tests. Each chapter concentrates on one of the four modules and offers 25 exercises that cover all the required skills. Every exercise also indicates the skill set that is being tested. Answers are provided to show the results you should obtain and, in many cases, the methods by which you will achieve a correct solution.

ECDL Advanced does not require the use of any particular named software, but the material in this book is based on PCs running the commonly available Microsoft Office XP (2002) version. You will also need an image editing program such as Paint Shop Pro or PhotoShop to carry out some of the presentation exercises.

All the files you need are on the accompanying CD. In most cases, you can open them and use Save As to create a copy that you can work with. For databases, first copy the closed files onto your computer. If any files remain Read-Only, right click the filename, select Properties and take off the tick in the attributes box.

In the syllabus, the ECDL Advanced Modules are labelled AM3, AM4, AM5 and AM6. The numbers of any learning outcomes being addressed in the book are shown in the form AM3.1.2.

About the author

Jackie Sherman has been involved in teaching and assessing IT courses at further education colleges since 1996. She also trains staff in an education department and writes courses for distance learning colleges. Her online activities include being on the National Tutor Database for LearnDirect and answering IT questions for the YouCanDoIT column for www.laterlife.com. Jackie is ECDL-qualified and is the author of many successful IT books.

Module AM3: Word Processing, Advanced Level

This module will test your ability to produce complex documents containing columns, section breaks or forms; use automated features such as macros or auto text; carry out calculations in tables; import objects; customize printing; apply advanced formats and protect your work.

EXERCISES 1 AND 2

You will need to know how to:

▶ Apply text effect options

▶ Apply animated text effect options

▶ Use automatic text entry options

▶ Apply automatic text formatting options

⟨ECDL⟩ **AM3.1.1**

Exercise 1

1. Start a new document and type the following text exactly as shown, making sure the automatic formatting option that formats ordinals (1st, 2nd, 3rd, etc.) as superscript is turned on:

   The Writing Studio
   It was 2nd January when I first ventured out into the snow. It felt like –50°C and the wind was whistling past my ears as I made my way up the road to the village.

2. Apply an animated text effect to the word whistling.

3. Take off the automatic formatting option for ordinals and type the next sentence after a clear line space:

   Three days earlier, on 30th December, things had been different.

4. Create an autotext entry for the phrase The Writing Studio.

5. Now insert this autotext entry automatically at the end of the document and apply a small caps font effect and double underline.

6. Apply a shadow to the word wind.

7. Save the document as *Wind* and close the file.

ANSWER 1

```
The Writing Studio

It was 2ⁿᵈ January when I first ventured out into the
snow.  It felt like -50°C and the wind was whistling
past my ears as I made my way up the road to the
village.

Three days earlier, on 30th December, things had been
different.

THE WRITING STUDIO
```

3

Exercise 2 1. Start a new document and type the address as set out below:

> Splendid Theatre
> Worthing Pier
> Sussex

2. Apply an emboss effect.

3. Create an autotext entry based on the address and then delete the original address from your document.

4. Now type the following:

> "King Lear" by William Shakespeare.

5. Take off the autoformat that replaces straight quotes with smart quotes (or reverse the effect if it was not on) and type the following on a new line:

> "Alice in Wonderland" by Lewis Carroll

6. Leave a clear line space and then recall the theatre address autotext entry you created earlier.

7. Select the word **Sussex** and apply any animation effect.

8. Save and close the document.

ANSWER 2

```
"King Lear" by William Shakespeare
"Alice in Wonderland" by Lewis Carroll
```

> Splendid Theatre
> Worthing Pier
> Sussex

EXERCISE 3

You will need to know how to:

- Use paragraph border options
- Apply paragraph shading
- Create styles
- Modify styles
- Wrap text round an image
- Apply widow and orphan controls

AM3.1.1 & AM3.1.2

1. Open the file *Calories*.

2. Apply Heading 1 style to the title **CALORIES**.

3. Create a new style of: Courier size 14, italic, and name it **Subheading**. Apply it to the three subheadings.

4. Save the document as *Calories2* and print one copy.

5. Now select the subheading **What is a Calorie?** Modify the **Subheading** style so that the font is Times New Roman. Update the document so that all the subheadings now reflect this modified style.

6. Shade the subheadings a light grey.

7. Border the title with a double line style, making sure the border extends across the width of the page.

8. Centre the title on the page.

9. Insert the picture *Bread* into the paragraph headed **What Calories Do.**

10. Apply a text wrap so that the picture is positioned to the right of the text.

11. Ensure that the last line of the paragraph and the subheading **How They Provide Energy** would never appear on a page by themselves.

12. Check that this formatting is applied by increasing the size of the picture slowly until the last line of the paragraph just moves over onto a new page.

13. Continue to increase the picture size until the complete paragraph including the subheading is on page 2.

14. Print a copy of the amended document.

15. Save and close the file

ANSWER 3

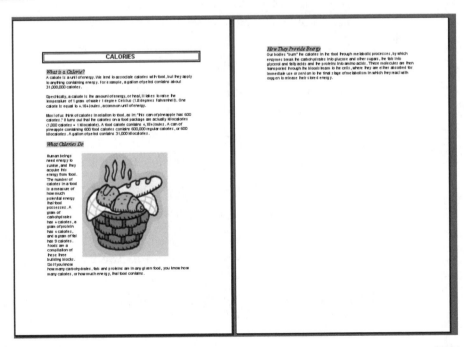

You will need to know how to:

- Use automatic text correction options
- Use text orientation options
- Insert and edit text boxes
- Apply border and shading options to text boxes
- Link text boxes

 AM3.1.1 & AM3.4.3

Exercise 4

1. Type the following text:

   GOING ON A JOURNEY

   Everyone needs a list of things to check before going away, to make sure they don't forget something vital. These are the items at the top of my list:

2. Change the automatic correction options so that the first letter of every sentence is *not* capitalized. Now type the following list:

   tickets
   passport
   health and travel insurance
   money
   language and guide books
   details of flights and destinations

3. Add a text box at the bottom of the document and enter the words: TRAVELLING ABROAD.

4. Re-orientate this text so that it reads vertically downwards and position it so that it is centrally aligned.

5. Resize it so that the words fit exactly on one line.

6. Move the box so that it is on the left of the document text.

7. Border the text box with a dark colour and add a coloured fill.

8. Save the file as *Going on a journey*.

9. Now add another text box at the bottom of the document and enter the names of the following countries in the form of a list: Australia, New Zealand, USA, Scotland, Wales, Cyprus, India and Switzerland.

10. Resize the box so that all the names fit comfortably inside.

11. Link this box to a second text box positioned alongside.

12. In the first text box, add the title: COUNTRIES I HAVE VISITED. Part of the list should now automatically appear in the second box.

13. Resize both boxes until there are four country names in each box.

14. Save and then close the amended file.

ANSWER 4

GOING ON A JOURNEY

Everyone needs a list of things to check before going away, to make sure they don't forget something vital. These are the items at the top of my list:
tickets
passport
health and travel insurance
money
language and guide books
details of flights and destinations

COUNTRIES I HAVE VISITED:
Australia
New Zealand
USA
Scotland

Wales
Cyprus
India
Switzerland

1

Exercise 5 1. Start a new document.

2. Turn off the automatic correction for two initial capitals and then type the following text:

When using the automatic text corrections, you will find that TYping ERrors such as these will be corrected automatically.

Here are the general corrections that are made.

3. Create a text box and enter the following rules, sizing the box so that it is just large enough to display the full text:

Two initial capitals
Capitals at the start of each sentence
Initial capitals for the names of days

4. Create a second text box underneath the first and link the two boxes.

5. Try to add the following rule into the first box without enlarging it. It should start in the second box automatically:

Correct accidental use of Caps Lock

6. Now copy the heading Here are the general corrections that are made into the first box and make sure that the third rule moves into the second box.

7. Format the heading to bold, size 14 and make changes to text box sizes so that there are two rules in each box.

8. Change the text orientation in both boxes so that text reads downwards. Amend the box sizes so that you can read the text clearly.

9. Move the boxes so that they are next to one another.

10. Format the boxes so that they have a thick border and colour fill.

11. Save as *Rules* and close the file.

5a – step 6

Here are the general
corrections that are made

Two initial capitals

Capitals at the start of each
sentence

Initial capitals for the names of
days

Correct accidental use of Caps
Lock

5b – step 10

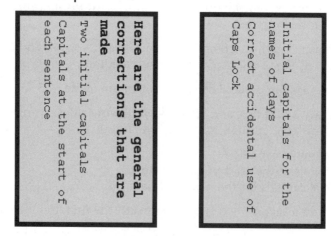

You will need to know how to:

- ◗ Create a new template
- ◗ Edit a template
- ◗ Create footnotes
- ◗ Modify existing footnotes

◊ECDL◊ **AM3.1.3 & AM3.3.3**

1. Locate any memo template and use it to create a new template.

2. Remove the option to send a copy (it may be labelled C.C.).

3. In the *From:* box, type: Sandra Deeds, Human Resources Director.

4. Choose new wording for the label of the *Re:* box, e.g. call it *Subject* or *Reason for Writing,* etc.

5. Give the memo the subject: Annual Appraisals.

6. Add the following text in the main area:

    As you know, we have introduced an Annual Appraisal Scheme and you are now being invited to attend an appraisal. Please bring along any details of training courses attended since your last appraisal and feel free to raise any issues of concern.

    Appraisal Details:

7. Click after the subject Annual Appraisals and insert the following footnote (numbered 1): Previously known as Annual Reviews.

8. Change page layout to landscape orientation.

9. Save the template as *Annual Appraisals* and print a copy before closing the file.

10. Now re-open the template. [If that is not possible, create a new template based on the original and save it as *Annual Appraisals2* at the end of the exercise.] Make the following changes:

    a. Sandra's name should be changed to Sheila.

    b. Amend the footnote relating to appraisals so that it reads: Previously known as Termly Reviews.

    c. Click next to the word Director and create a new footnote: Appointment confirmed last week.

    d. Add a final footnote after the words Appraisal Scheme: For those with over 1 year's service.

    e. Change the format of the numbering of the footnotes from 1, 2, 3 to i, ii, iii.

Save and close the amended template.

6a – step 8

6b

From: Sheila Deeds, Human Resources Director[i]

Date:

Subject: Annual Appraisals[ii]

As you know, we have introduced an Annual Appraisal
of training courses attended since your last appraisal and

Appraisal Details:

[i] Appointment confirmed last week
[ii] Previously known as Termly Reviews
[iii] For those with over 1 year's service

EXERCISES 7 AND 8

You will need to know how to:

◗ Create multiple column layouts

- Modify columns

- Insert and delete column breaks

<ECDL> **AM3.2.4**

Exercise 7
1. Open the file *Banbury*.

2. Set the main text in two equal columns with a line between.

3. The second column should start with the text: However, it was the Saxons …

4. Centre the title above both columns of text and increase it to font size 14.

5. Save as *Banbury1*.

6. Now change the format to three columns with the last column slightly wider than the other two. Remove the lines between columns.

7. Delete the original column break and introduce two more, so that column 2 starts with The site contained … and column 3 starts with Banbury stands at the junction …

8. Close up any spaces between paragraphs.

9. Add the following text, formatted in bold, at the bottom of the columns, making sure it extends across the width of the page: Ride a cock horse to Banbury Cross, to see a fine lady ride on a white horse. With rings on her fingers and bells on her toes, she shall have music wherever she goes.

10. Save the file as *Banbury2* and then close the file.

7a – step 4

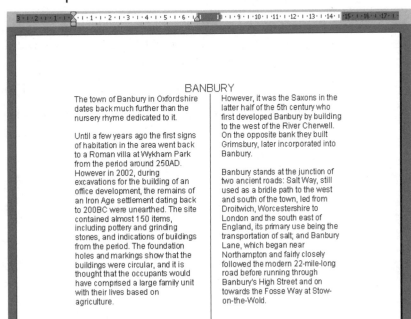

BANBURY

The town of Banbury in Oxfordshire dates back much further than the nursery rhyme dedicated to it.

Until a few years ago the first signs of habitation in the area went back to a Roman villa at Wykham Park from the period around 250AD. However in 2002, during excavations for the building of an office development, the remains of an Iron Age settlement dating back to 200BC were unearthed. The site contained almost 150 items, including pottery and grinding stones, and indications of buildings from the period. The foundation holes and markings show that the buildings were circular, and it is thought that the occupants would have comprised a large family unit with their lives based on agriculture.

However, it was the Saxons in the latter half of the 5th century who first developed Banbury by building to the west of the River Cherwell. On the opposite bank they built Grimsbury, later incorporated into Banbury.

Banbury stands at the junction of two ancient roads: Salt Way, still used as a bridle path to the west and south of the town, led from Droitwich, Worcestershire to London and the south east of England, its primary use being the transportation of salt; and Banbury Lane, which began near Northampton and fairly closely followed the modern 22-mile-long road before running through Banbury's High Street and on towards the Fosse Way at Stow-on-the-Wold.

7b

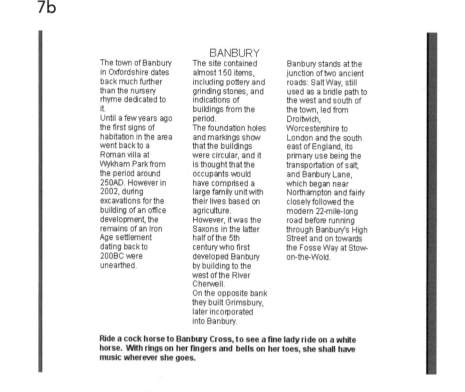

BANBURY

The town of Banbury in Oxfordshire dates back much further than the nursery rhyme dedicated to it.

Until a few years ago the first signs of habitation in the area went back to a Roman villa at Wykham Park from the period around 250AD. However in 2002, during excavations for the building of an office development, the remains of an Iron Age settlement dating back to 200BC were unearthed.

The site contained almost 150 items, including pottery and grinding stones, and indications of buildings from the period.

The foundation holes and markings show that the buildings were circular, and it is thought that the occupants would have comprised a large family unit with their lives based on agriculture.

However, it was the Saxons in the latter half of the 5th century who first developed Banbury by building to the west of the River Cherwell.

On the opposite bank they built Grimsbury, later incorporated into Banbury.

Banbury stands at the junction of two ancient roads: Salt Way, still used as a bridle path to the west and south of the town, led from Droitwich, Worcestershire to London and the south east of England, its primary use being the transportation of salt; and Banbury Lane, which began near Northampton and fairly closely followed the modern 22-mile-long road before running through Banbury's High Street and on towards the Fosse Way at Stow-on-the-Wold.

Ride a cock horse to Banbury Cross, to see a fine lady ride on a white horse. With rings on her fingers and bells on her toes, she shall have music wherever she goes.

Exercise 8

1. Open the file *Cleaning*.

2. Set the main text in two columns of unequal width. Insert a column break so that the second column starts with the words It makes light work ...

3. Add a line between columns.

4. Add the following at the end of the text so that it stretches across the full width of the page: Phone us on 0800 3345556 and we will deliver your vacuum cleaner direct to your home anywhere in the UK.

5. Now change the column widths so that they are equal and remove the line.

6. Remove the column break and make sure the second column starts with the words The *Varrum Featherlite* needs no dust bags ...

7. Save these changes and close the file.

8a – step 4

NEW LIGHTWEIGHT VACUUM CLEANER

If you are tired of dragging a heavy machine around your house from room to room, then try the amazing, new, lightweight *Varrum Featherlite* free in your home for 5 days.

Up to ten times lighter than other upright cleaners the *Varrum Featherlite* will have an instant effect on your household chores.

It makes light work of any cleaning job and you will work five times faster due to its super suction power.

The *Varrum Featherlite* needs no dust bags – empty it straight into the waste bin and never run out when you have a cleaning job to do.

So lightweight, the *Varrum Featherlite* converts to a multi-purpose hand vac for quick hoovering of curtains, upholstery and those hard-to-reach areas.

Money back guarantee if not completely satisfied. Send off for your free trial today!

Phone us on 0800 3345556 and we will deliver your vacuum cleaner direct to your home anywhere in the UK.

8b – step 6

NEW LIGHTWEIGHT VACUUM CLEANER

If you are tired of dragging a heavy machine around your house from room to room, then try the amazing, new, lightweight *Varrum Featherlite* free in your home for 5 days.

Up to ten times lighter than other upright cleaners the *Varrum Featherlite* will have an instant effect on your household chores.

It makes light work of any cleaning job and you will work five times faster due to its super suction power.

The *Varrum Featherlite* needs no dust bags – empty it straight into the waste bin and never run out when you have a cleaning job to do.

So lightweight, the *Varrum Featherlite* converts to a multi-purpose hand vac for quick hoovering of curtains, upholstery and those hard-to-reach areas.

Money back guarantee if not completely satisfied. Send off for your free trial today!

Phone us on 0800 3345556 and we will deliver your vacuum cleaner direct to your home anywhere in the UK.

EXERCISES 9 AND 10

You will need to know how to:

▶ Convert tabbed text into a table

▶ Merge table cells

▶ Sort data in a table

▶ Perform calculations on table contents

Exercise 9
1. Open the file *Gifts*.
2. Convert the tabbed text into a table.
3. Insert a new first row and add the entry: RECENT GIFT PURCHASES.
4. Format this text to bold, italic, font size 14.
5. Merge the first row cells and centre the title above the table contents.
6. Sort the table contents alphabetically by Item.
7. Add a new row at the bottom of the table. In the first cell, enter the words: Overall Total.
8. Use a formula to calculate the total cost of all the items and enter this at the bottom of the TOTAL column.
9. Print a copy of the table.
10. Now make the following amendment: the UNIT COST of Local honey is £3 and so the TOTAL for honey should be £18.
11. Update the Overall Total to take account of this change.
12. Print a final copy of the table and then save and close the file.

9a – step 8

RECENT GIFT PURCHASES			
ITEM	NUMBER	UNIT COST	TOTAL
Box of fudge	10	£1.50	£15
Local honey	6	£2	£12
Magazine	4	£3.20	£12.80
Postcard	5	£0.80	£4
Tray	1	£9.50	£9.50
Overall Total			£53.30

9b

RECENT GIFT PURCHASES			
ITEM	NUMBER	UNIT COST	TOTAL
Box of fudge	10	£1.50	£15
Local honey	6	£3	£18
Magazine	4	£3.20	£12.80
Postcard	5	£0.80	£4
Tray	1	£9.50	£9.50
Overall Total			£59.30

Exercise 10
1. Open the document *Hours worked*.
2. Convert the tabbed text into a table.

3. Merge the bottom cells so that **TOTAL** appears across four columns. Centre the word **TOTAL** in the cell.

4. Use a calculation to total the **CLAIM** column.

5. Amend column widths so that all entries are displayed on a single line.

6. Sort the data in descending order of **CLAIMS**.

7. The rate per hour for **Proofreading** has increased to £20 per hour so the Claim for work on 3/7/06 should now show £140. Make these changes to the table data and update the final total.

8. Save and close the file.

10a – step 5

Date	Work	Hours	Rate per hour	CLAIM
3/7/06	Proofreading	7	£15	£105
8/7/06	Liaising with author	14	£10	£140
12/8/06	Checking 2nd draft	25	£15	£375
24/8/06	Writing introduction	8	£15	£120
TOTAL				£740.00

10b

Date	Work	Hours	Rate per hour	CLAIM
12/8/06	Checking 2nd draft	25	£15	£375
8/7/06	Liaising with author	14	£10	£140
24/8/06	Writing introduction	8	£15	£120
3/7/06	Proofreading	7	£20	£140
TOTAL				£775.00

EXERCISES 11 AND 12

You will need to know how to:

- Create a simple drawing
- Use pre-defined shapes
- Send shapes to the front or back of another shape
- Send shapes behind or in front of text
- Group or ungroup shapes

Exercise 11 1. Create a drawing of a landscape similar to the one shown that includes two trees each made up of at least two shapes, a lake and some mountains. Try to use a mixture of lines, ovals, rectangles and pre-defined shapes.

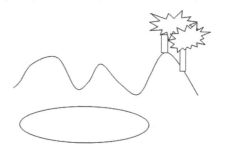

2. Group the trees and move them to the top of the *left*-hand mountain.

3. Add a pre-defined shape to represent the sun and position it so that the lower half is *behind* the trees.

4. Ungroup the trees.

5. Regroup one tree, reduce it in size and move it to beside the lake.

6. Now add a text box with no visible border that contains the text Tranquillity formatted in bold and italic.

7. Position this across the mountain range, making sure the mountains are not obscured by any of the text box border.

8. Below the picture, type the words **But where is the boat?** in font size 20. Centre the text on the page.

9. Group the entire picture and move it down the page so that it covers the words. Send it behind the text so that the words appear across the lake (see answer for correct position).

10. Save the document as *Mountains*.

ANSWER 11

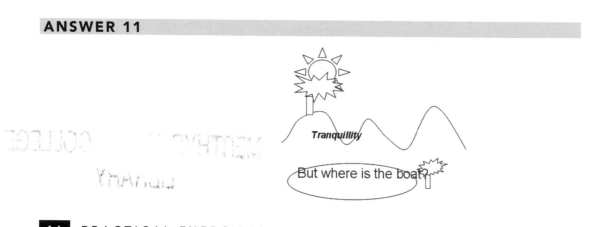

Exercise 12 1. Create a flower drawing similar to the one shown, using AutoShapes.

2. Colour the petals red, the centre of the flower yellow and the stem and leaves green.

3. Group the shapes and reduce the drawing in size.

4. Draw a large star and colour it pale yellow.

5. Position it behind the flower.

6. Enter the words First Prize somewhere on the page. Format them to bold, size 14.

7. Group the flower with the star and drag this drawing across the wording.

8. Re-order the drawing so that the words are visible – try to position it so the words are across the centre of the flower.

9. Save as *Flower* and close the file.

ANSWER 12

EXERCISE 13

You will need to know how to:

♦ Create a table of contents

♦ Update a table of contents

- Format a table of contents
- Create and edit an index
- Print a defined selection

AM3.2.2, AM3.3.1 & AM3.6.1

1. Open the file *Bees*.

2. Apply a top level Heading 1 style to the title.

3. Apply a Heading 2 style to the three subheadings: Honey Bees, Errors When Siting Beehives on Allotments and Things to Do.

4. Create a table of contents at the beginning of the document, above the title, based on the title and subheadings.

5. Print page 1 of the document only.

6. Create the following subheadings: Varroa Mites above the second paragraph; Contribution Made by Bees above the third paragraph; Don't above the fourth paragraph; and Best Practice above the final paragraph.

7. Create a new style that differs from Headings 1 and 2, e.g. Arial font size 14, italic. Name it New Subheading and apply it to these subheadings.

8. Update the table of contents to include these new subheadings.

9. Select and apply a different format to the table of contents.

10. Change the wording of the subheading Errors When Siting Beehives on Allotments so that it reads: Beehives on Allotments.

11. Make sure the table of contents is updated to take this change into account.

12. At the end of the document, on a new page, set up an index that contains the following words: Honey bees, Varroa mite, flight path and emergency.

13. Give the index a title and apply Heading 2 style. Update the table of contents to take this extra entry into account.

14. Now mark the word pollination and add it to the index. Update the index.

15. Select and print only the updated table of contents and index.

16. Save and close the file.

13a – step 5

KEEPING BEES ON ALLOTMENTS

Honey Bees

Honey bees are insects that have been on Earth for about 100 million years, well before any humans. Bees thrived without the help of man and still do in some parts of the world. At the beginning of the 20th century disease caused

13b – final table of contents

13c – final index

Index

EXERCISE 14

You will need to know how to:

- Record a simple macro
- Run a macro
- Copy a macro
- Assign a macro to a custom button on the toolbar
- Add a watermark to a document

1. Start a new blank document.

2. Record a macro named **Poster** that changes the orientation to landscape, adds today's date as a header and the text **Poster** as a footer. Store it in the current document.

3. Copy the macro to the Normal template.

4. Assign the macro to a button on the toolbar.

5. Close the document.

6. Start a new document and run the macro.

7. Now type the following details for a poster. Enlarge and emphasize the text and centre it on the page:

THE GREATEST SHOW ON EARTH

Reggie's Circus is coming to town

See the animals, jugglers and clowns

Come to the Green on Saturday, 15th September

Half price tickets for the first lucky 25 people

8. Find an appropriate clipart picture and use this to create a watermark behind the text. Make sure it fills most of the page.

9. Save and close the document.

14a – step 6

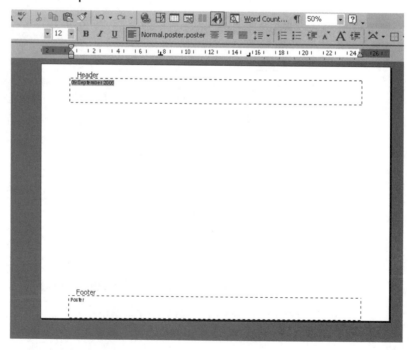

14b

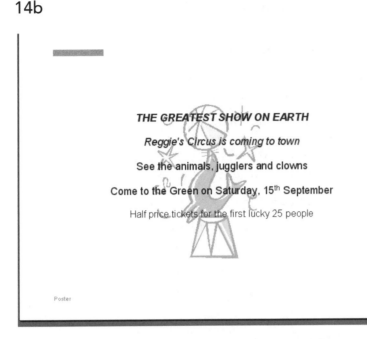

EXERCISE 15

You will need to know how to:

◆ Modify image borders

◆ Apply numbered captions to an image

◆ Add or update captions

◆ Use automatic caption options.

◆ Print a defined number of pages per sheet.

AM3.4.5, AM3.4.6 & AM3.6.1

1. Open the document *Making a cake*.

2. Border the first image with a thick line.

3. Border the second image with a different style of line.

4. Select the first image and insert a caption. It should be labelled Cooking, with the caption: Collect requirements.

5. Add the caption Fresh Eggs to the second image and Finished Cake to the third image.

6. Add the following text at the end of step 4: If you have made small cakes, keep them in their bun cases but turn them out as soon as possible.

7. Insert the image file *Small cakes*.

8. Add the caption Small cakes, and make sure all the document caption numbers are updated.

9. Turn on the automatic caption option. At the end of the document, add a new step 6 and enter the text: Here are a few cake decoration ideas. Now insert image files *Cake 1* and *Cake 2* and make sure captions are added automatically.

10. Change the style of border for image 1.

11. Delete image 2 together with the caption, close up the space and make sure all the document caption numbers are updated.

12. Print both pages of the document on one sheet.

13. Save and close the file.

15a – step 9

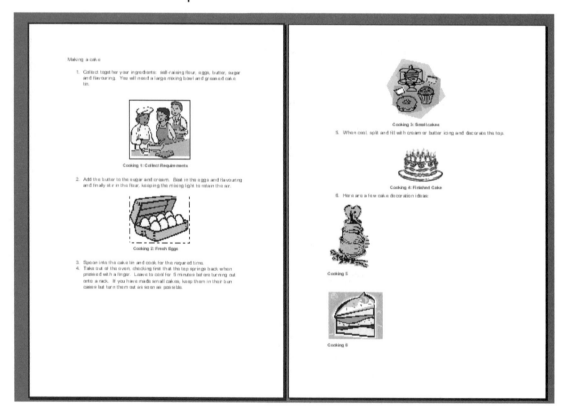

15b – step 10 – amended border and updated captions

Cooking 1: Collect Requirements

2. Add the butter to the sugar and cream. Beat in the eggs and flavouring and finally stir in the flour, keeping the mixing light to retain the air.
3. Spoon into the cake tin and cook for the required time.
4. Take out of the oven, checking first that the top springs back when pressed with a finger. Leave to cool for 5 minutes before turning out onto a rack. If you have made small cakes, keep them in their bun cases but turn them out as soon as possible.

Cooking 2: Small cakes

5. When cool, split and fill with cream or butter icing and decorate the top.

Cooking 3: Finished Cake

EXERCISE 16

You will need to know how to:

▶ Edit a mail merge data source

▶ Sort data source records

▶ Merge a document with a data source using given merge criteria

 AM3.5.1

1. Open the file *Theatre members* and change the **Price** entry for Daisy Harris to £5.

2. Sort the records alphabetically by surname and then save and close the file.

3. Open the file *Theatre information* and link it to *Theatre members*.

4. Display Daisy Harris's record and check that the **Price** shows as £5.

5. Now merge the document with all the records that include **Senior** membership. There should be only two records selected.

6. Merge to a new document saved as *Seniors*.

7. Print *Seniors* showing both records on one page.

8. Carry out a new mail merge selecting only **Junior** members living in **Leeds**. You should find only one record is selected.

9. Close all files.

16a – step 4

Daisy Harris

Dear Daisy

As a Junior member of the Friends of Hayfield Theatre, we are writing to inform you that, this year, your tickets will only cost £5

We hope to see you at many of our productions and have pleasure in enclosing the programme for the coming season.

With Best Wishes

Georgina Brinks
Theatre Manager

16b – Seniors

Don Bradford

Dear Don

As a Senior member of the Friends of Hayfield Theatre, we are writing to inform you that, this year, your tickets will only cost £15

We hope to see you at many of our productions and have pleasure in enclosing the programme for the coming season.

With Best Wishes

Georgina Brinks
Theatre Manager

Harold James

Dear Harold

As a Senior member of the Friends of Hayfield Theatre, we are writing to inform you that, this year, your tickets will only cost £15

We hope to see you at many of our productions and have pleasure in enclosing the programme for the coming season.

With Best Wishes

Georgina Brinks
Theatre Manager

EXERCISE 17

You will need to know how to:

▶ Add or remove text comments

- Edit text comments
- Track changes in a document
- Accept or reject changes
- Create or delete section breaks
- Add or delete a bookmark

AM3.1.4, AM3.2.3 & AM3.3.1

1. Open the file *Brunel*.

2. Add a comment to the figure 35 on page 2: **This should be 27.**

3. Edit the comment attached to the word **Monkwearmouth** in the second paragraph by adding: **This is correct.**

4. Reject the change to the word **Controversially.**

5. Insert a section break after the words **made 60 crossings.**

6. Insert a bookmark named **bridge** at the beginning of the second paragraph.

7. Delete the bookmark named **station.**

8. Remove the comment **Do we have a picture?** attached to **the Maidenhead Bridge.**

9. Update the file to save the changes and then close the file.

17a – showing added comment and rejected change to a word

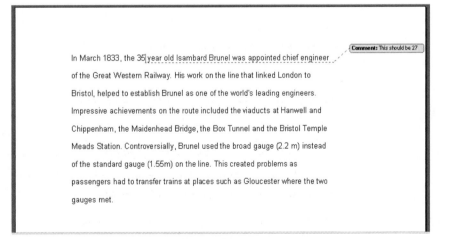

PART 1 MODULE AM3: WORD PROCESSING, ADVANCED LEVEL **25**

17b – *bridge* bookmark added, *station* removed

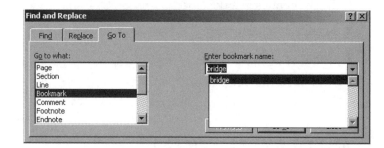

You will need to know how to:

▶ Use outline options

▶ Create a cross-reference

 AM3.1.2 & AM3.3.1

Exercise 18 1. Start a new document and type the following list:

Healthy Living
Food
Eat 5 fruit or vegetables a day
Avoid fatty foods
Limit alcohol intake
Exercise
Take regular exercise
Walk or cycle instead of taking the car
Lifestyle
Give up smoking
Avoid sweets, cakes and biscuits

2. Promote the first line, Healthy Living, to level 1.

3. Demote the lines Food and Exercise to level 2.

4. Demote all other lines to level 3.

5. Now promote the line Lifestyle to level 2.

6. Move the entry Avoid sweets, cakes and biscuits so that it becomes the 4th item in the paragraph headed Food.

7. Move the entire Food paragraph so that it will appear in the document after the Lifestyle paragraph.

8. In normal view, add the following text on a new line after Healthy Living: Now we are more aware of what to do to stay healthy, the government has started to produce booklets that you can find in shops, especially supermarkets.

9. Type the word See: and then insert a cross-reference to the heading Eat 5 fruit or vegetables a day.

10. Save the file as *Lifestyle* and print a copy.

18a – step 4

◊ **Healthy Living**
   ◊ *Food*
         □ **Eat 5 fruit or vegetables a day**
         □ **Avoid fatty foods**
         □ **Limit alcohol intake**
   ◊ *Exercise*
         □ **Take regular exercise**
         □ **Walk or cycle instead of taking the car**
         □ **Lifestyle**
         □ **Give up smoking**
         □ **Avoid sweets, cakes and biscuits**

18b

Healthy Living

Now we are more aware of what to do to stay healthy, the government has started to produce booklets that you can find in shops, especially supermarkets. See: **Eat 5 fruit or vegetables a day**

Exercise

Take regular exercise

Walk or cycle instead of taking the car

Lifestyle

Give up smoking

Food

Eat 5 fruit or vegetables a day

Avoid fatty foods

Limit alcohol intake

Avoid sweets, cakes and biscuits

Exercise 19 1. Open the file *Book*.

2. Show only level 1 in outline view.

3. Move Having Fun so that it becomes the first section after Introduction.

4. Promote Tim phones to a level 1 heading.

5. Move the entry Fanfare Carnivals hit town to become the first item under Having Fun.

6. Insert page breaks so that each level 1 heading starts on a new page and you have a six-page document.

7. Number the pages.

8. In normal view, click after Mark receives the bad news and type: See Mark calls. Add a cross-reference to this heading that will display the page number and the text **on page** ... .

9. Save and close the file.

19a – step 5

- **Introduction**
- **Having Fun**
  - *Fanfare Carnivals hit town*
  - *Mary and Hugo lose their money*
  - *All three go to the fair*
- **The Journey**
  - *Mark receives the bad news*
  - *Jessie goes to the airport*
  - *The plane is cancelled for 12 hours*
  - *Mark meets Jessie in the hotel foyer*
- **The Worst Possible Moment**
  - *Audrey decides to have a bath*
  - *Mark rushes back home for his keys*
- **Tim phones**
- **Across the Continents**
  - *Halima receives the letter*
    - Her father is ill
    - Aswad is away
  - *She decides not to reply*
  - *Mark calls*
  - *Halima leaves for Egypt*

19b – step 8

The Journey

Mark receives the bad news
See Mark calls: on page 6

Jessie goes to the airport

The plane is cancelled for 12 hours

Mark meets Jessie in the hotel foyer

You will need to know how to:

▸ Insert a field code

▸ Edit or update a field code entry

▸ Lock or unlock a field code

▸ Split cells in a table

▸ Print odd or even pages only

◊ECDL◊ **AM3.3.2, AM3.4.1 & AM3.6.1**

Exercise 20 1. Open the file *Field codes document*.

2. Split the cell containing the text Today's Date so that there are two columns. Repeat this split for the cell containing the text Time of Editing Table.

3. Insert a date field into the empty cell next to Today's Date.

4. Insert a time field into the empty cell next to Time of Editing Table.

5. Lock this field so the time cannot be updated.

6. Save the file as *Amended Field codes*.

7. Update the file name field showing in the header.

8. Edit the date so that it has a different format.

9. Insert a new field in the header showing Page 1 of 1.

10. Insert a section break below the table to create a second page. The page number field should update automatically.

11. Unlock the time field and update the time showing in the table.

12. Save the document.

13. Print odd pages of the document only.

20a – step 5

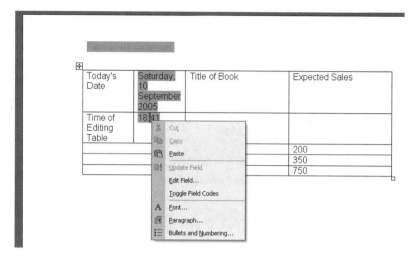

Today's Date	Saturday, 10 September 2005	Title of Book	Expected Sales
Time of Editing Table	18:41		
			200
			350
			750

Cut
Copy
Paste
Update Field
Edit Field…
Toggle Field Codes
Font…
Paragraph…
Bullets and Numbering…

20b – step 7

Header
Amended field codes

Today's Date	September	Title of Book	Expected Sales
Time of Editing Table			
		Blue Moon	200
		Rapid Fire	350
		Sweet Hopes	750

20c

Amended field codes   Page 1 of 2

Today's Date	10/09/05	Title of Book	E
Time of	18:59		

Exercise 21 1. Start a new document and create the following table.

Students	Work	Date in	Mark
Harry Smith	Essay 1	2/7/06	68%
Sally Fields	Essay 2	2/7/06	55%
Tyron Dales	Exercise 4	14/8/06	75%

2. Split the cell containing the heading Work and add the entry Summer School.

3. Add a field below the table that will count the number of words in your document. Label it: Word count.

4. Save the file as *Students*.

5. Below the word count, add a field that will display the file name.

6. Save a new version of the file as *Students – Summer School*.

7. Update the file name field.

8. Lock the word count field.

9. Add the following entry to the table: Steven Harris, Final project, date in: 22/8/06, mark 85%.

10. Try to update the word count.

11. Now unlock the field and update the entry.

12. Create a page break at the end of the table and print only even pages of your document.

13. Save and close the file.

21a – step 5

Students	Work	Summer School	Date in	Mark
Harry Smith	Essay 1		2/7/06	68%
Sally Fields	Essay 2		2/7/06	55%
Tyron Dales	Exercise 4		14/8/06	75%

Word count: 28

Students

21b

Students	Work	Summer School	Date in	Mark
Harry Smith	Essay 1		2/7/06	68%
Sally Fields	Essay 2		2/7/06	55%
Tyron Dales	Exercise 4		14/8/06	75%
Steven Harris	Final project		22/8/06	85%

Word count: 38

Students - Summer School

You will need to know how to:

▶ Add password protection to a document

▶ Remove password protection

▶ Modify an embedded worksheet

▶ Create a chart from a table

▶ Modify chart formatting

▶ Position a chart in a document

 AM3.3.4 & AM3.4.4

1. Open the file *Survey*. It is password protected, so you will need to use the password **cars**.

2. Remove the password protection from the document.

3. The embedded worksheet labelled *Results of Survey* needs to be amended:

    a. Change the make of car from **Mini** to **Fiesta**.

    b. Increase the number of **black Toyota** cars to **12**.

    c. Add a new record on the next row: **Polo** with **0 red** or **blue** cars, **3 silver** and **2 black**.

4. Return to the document and ensure that all the spreadsheet data is fully displayed.

5. Save the file as *Updated survey* and password protect. Use the password **update** and check that it works.

6. Now create a 2-D column chart based on the table headed *Preferences*.

7. Make sure the features and not votes are displayed along the X-axis.

8. Remove the legend and increase the size of the chart so that all features are clearly visible.

9. Add a chart title: **Preferred Features**.

10. Label the X-axis **Features** and the Y-axis **Votes**.

11. Print a copy of the document.

12. Now move the chart to a new position, e.g. above the table of data headed *Preferences*.

13. Finally, change the chart type to a Pie chart and add data labels and a legend. Format the various elements as you like.

14. Save and close the updated document.

22a – amended worksheet

Results of Survey

	Red	Blue	Silver	Black
Rover	0	2	7	4
Fiesta	2	1	0	6
Vauxhall	3	7	13	9
Renault	1	0	3	5
Toyota	3	4	8	12
Polo	0	0	3	2

22b – column chart

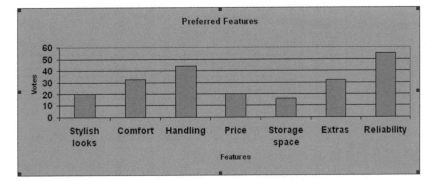

22c

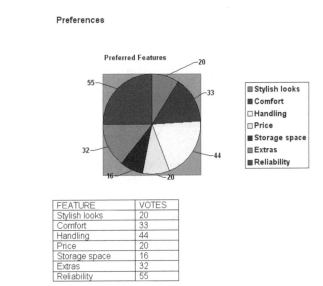

FEATURE	VOTES
Stylish looks	20
Comfort	33
Handling	44
Price	20
Storage space	16
Extras	32
Reliability	55

You will need to know how to:

- Create and edit a form
- Use various form field options
- Delete fields in a form
- Protect a form

 AM3.4.2

Exercise 23
1. Start a new document and insert a 2 × 6 table.

2. Add the following entries as set out below.

First name	
Surname	
Age on 31st December	
Vegetarian	
Airport	
Holiday during school term	Yes No

3. In the second column, to the right of **First name** and **Surname**, insert Text Form Fields.

4. To the right of **Age**, insert a Drop-Down Form Field that includes the following items: **Under 12, 13–60, Over 60**.

5. To the right of **Vegetarian**, insert a Drop-Down Form Field offering **Yes** and **No**.

6. To the right of **Airport**, insert a Drop-Down Form Field offering the items **Birmingham, Luton, Manchester** and **Gatwick**.

7. In the bottom cell, add a Check Box Field next to **Yes** and another next to **No**.

8. Protect the form and check that the fields work correctly.

9. Save as *Airport form*.

10. Change the heading **Surname** to **Last Name**.

11. Amend the drop-down list of airports by adding **Heathrow** and removing **Luton**. Move **Heathrow** so that it is the first choice in the list.

12. Delete the Drop-Down Form Field to the right of Vegetarian.

13. Save these changes and close the file.

23a – step 8

First name		
Surname		
Age on 31st December	Under 12	
Vegetarian	Yes	
Airport	Birmingham ▾	
Holiday during school term	Birmingham	No ☐
	Luton	
	Manchester	
	Gatwick	

23b

First name		
Last Name		
Age on 31st December	Under 12	
Vegetarian		
Airport	Heathrow	
Holiday during school term	Yes ☐	No ☐

Exercise 24 1. Create the following table:

Free Eye Check	
Eye Test	
Frames	
Contact lens fitting	
Payments	

2. In the second column, add a Check Box Form Field for Free Eye Check.

3. Add a Text Form Field for Eye Test.

4. Add a Drop-Down Form Field for Frames and enter the following choices: Gold, Silver, Brown, Black and Blue.

5. Create two more Drop-Down Form Fields: Contact lens fitting: Booked/ Not booked/Not interested, and Payments: Direct debit/Cash/Cheque/ Credit card.

6. Save the file as *Eyes*.

7. Protect the form and then use it to enter the following details:

Free Eye Check	Yes
Eye Test	12/10/06
Frames	Black
Contact lens fitting	Not booked
Payments	Credit card

8. Make the following changes:

   a. Frame choices should include **Red**.

   b. Move **Brown** up the list so that it is the first choice offered.

   c. Remove the **Direct Debit** payment option.

   d. Delete the Form Field for **Eye Test**.

9. Save and close the file.

24a – step 5

Free Eye Check	☐
Eye Test	
Frames	Gold
Contact lens fitting	Booked
Payments	Direct debit

24b

Free Eye Check	☒
Eye Test	
Frames	Brown
Contact lens fitting	Not booked
Payments	Cash ▾

Cash
Cheque
Credit card

EXERCISE 25

You will need to know how to:

- Create a new master document
- Create a sub-document based on styles in a master document
- Add or remove a sub-document within a master document

ECDL **AM3.2.1**

1. Start a new document in Outline View.

2. Type: **UK Education** at level 1.

3. Type the following headings at level 2:

Nursery Schools
Primary Schools
Secondary Schools
6th Form College
University

4. Type the following subheadings at level 3 under **Secondary Schools**:

Comprehensive
Grammar
Technical

5. Save the file as *Education*.

6. Create six sub-documents based on the level 2 headings.

7. Insert the sub-document *Further Education* between 6th Form College and University.

8. Remove the sub-document 6th Form College.

9. Save these changes and close the master document.

ANSWER 25

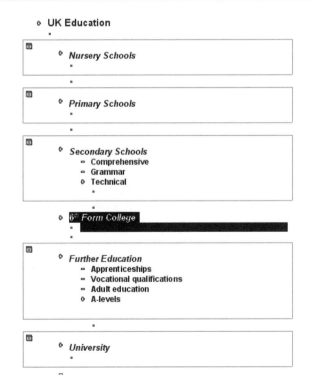

- UK Education

- Nursery Schools

- Primary Schools

- Secondary Schools
  - Comprehensive
  - Grammar
  - Technical

- 6th Form College

- Further Education
  - Apprenticeships
  - Vocational qualifications
  - Adult education
  - A-levels

- University

2

Module AM4: Spreadsheets, Advanced Level

You will be tested on your ability to create complex charts; link worksheets; use templates; analyze data using pivot tables or filters; customize forms and reports; use a variety of functions; create macros; apply advanced formats and protect your data.

You will need to know how to:

▶ Use a template

▶ Edit a template

[ECDL] **AM4.2.4**

1. Open the file *Invoice* and then save it as a template with the same name.

2. Locate and open the *Invoice* template and make the following changes:

   a. The name should be Peter Halstead.
   b. Tracing photographs should read Taking photographs.

3. Save the amended template with the same name to replace the original.

4. Now create a new spreadsheet based on the template. Add the following costs for this month:

   a. Proofreading – £300.
   b. Taking photographs – £150.
   c. Liaising with authors – £90.

5. Save as *Latest Invoice* and then close the file.

1

	A	B	C	D	E
1	INVOICE				
2					
3	From:	Peter Halstead		Date	29/06/2006
4					
5	**Work:**			Costs	
6	Proofreading manuscript			£300	
7	Taking photographs			£150	
8	Drawing cover picture				
9	Writing introduction				
10	Liaising with authors			£90	
11					
12					
13					
14	TOTAL			£540	
15					
16					

EXERCISES 2 AND 3

You will need to know how to:

▶ Name a cell range

▶ Create custom number formats

- Apply automatic formatting
- Freeze row or column headings

◊ECDL◊ **AM4.1.1 & AM4.1.2**

Exercise 2
1. Open the workbook *Cake sales*.

2. Name the cell range B3:B12 as **Cakes**.

3. Name the cell range C3:C12 as **Bakes**.

4. Name the cell range D3:D12 as **Biscuits**.

5. Using these names, enter formulae in the **TOTAL** row to total the sales of whole cakes, tray bakes and biscuits in April and May.

6. Format the first date in the **Week Ending** column so that it is displayed as: **01 April 06**. Copy this format down the column so that all dates appear in the same format.

7. Format the sales figures as currency with two decimal places, making sure the £ symbol is displayed.

8. Format the three totals in bold. Now apply a custom format to these cells to add the letter 'p' after the decimal places.

9. Apply an Autoformat that will add shading and borders to the data but not change the Number format options. If necessary, re-apply bold to the totals.

10. Freeze the column headings and then scroll down to row 100. In the Biscuits column, add the text: **No more sold after this date**.

11. Rename the sheet *Cakes* and then save and close the file.

2a – step 9

C13	▼	*fx* =SUM(Bakes)	

	A	B	C	D
1	CAKE SALES			
2	**Week Ending**	**Whole Cakes**	**Tray Bakes**	**Biscuits**
3	01 April 06	£24.35	£16.45	£9.40
4	08 April 06	£15.42	£13.67	£8.55
5	15 April 06	£26.06	£12.67	£7.42
6	22 April 06	£12.24	£14.85	£8.25
7	29 April 06	£9.65	£13.55	£9.50
8	06 May 06	£30.30	£11.62	£6.50
9	13 May 06	£18.69	£18.42	£7.12
10	20 May 06	£12.44	£15.40	£6.85
11	27 May 06	£26.78	£12.35	£5.20
12	03 June 06	£22.45	£19.22	£10.45
13	**TOTAL**	**£198.38p**	**£148.20p**	**£79.24p**

2b – step 10

	A	B	C	D	E	F
	cake sales					
1	CAKE SALES					
2	**Week Ending**	**Whole Cakes**	**Tray Bakes**	**Biscuits**		
98						
99						
100				No more sold after this date		
101						

Exercise 3

1. Open *Decorating*. This spreadsheet shows decorating costs as they were two years ago.

2. Name the cell range E3:E9 as Total.

3. Add the row heading Final price in A14 and work out the total for E3:E9 in B14. Use the name of the cell range in the formula.

4. Prices have now increased. In A15 enter the row heading Increase, and enter 5% in B15.

5. Use the value in B14 to work out the New total in row 16 (i.e. total plus 5% of that figure).

6. Format all prices to currency.

7. Freeze column headings and move to row 50. Under Cost (p.sq.m) enter the words All up by 5%.

8. Format the entries in the Size column to add the letters 'sq.m' after the numeric data.

9. Finally, apply a List Autoformat to the main spreadsheet data.

10. Save and close the file.

3a – step 6

B14   ▼   *fx* =SUM(Total)

	A	B	C	D	E
1	**CURTAINS**				
2	*Type*	*Room*	*Cost (p.sq.m)*	*Size (sq.m)*	*Final price*
3	**Flowered**	Study	£8.00	80	£640.00
4	**Woven**	Sitting	£15.75	95	£1,496.25
5	**Oak blinds**	Conservatory	£14.00	110	£1,540.00
6	**Paisley**	Dining	£26.00	125	£3,250.00
7	**Stars**	Bedroom 1	£7.50	45	£337.50
8	**Linen**	Bedroom 2	£6.00	140	£840.00
9	**Jack & Jill**	Nursery	£12.00	40	£480.00
10					
11					
12					
13					
14	Final price	£8,583.75			
15	Increase	5%			
16	New total	£9,012.94			

3b

	A	B	C	D	E
1	*CURTAINS*				
2	*Type*	*Room*	*Cost (p.sq.m)*	*Size (sq.m)*	*Final price*
3	Flowered	Study	£8.00	80 sq.m	£640.00
4	Woven	Sitting	£15.75	95 sq.m	£1,496.25
5	Oak blinds	Conservatory	£14.00	110 sq.m	£1,540.00
6	Paisley	Dining	£26.00	125 sq.m	£3,250.00
7	Stars	Bedroom 1	£7.50	45 sq.m	£337.50
8	Linen	Bedroom 2	£6.00	140 sq.m	£840.00
9	Jack & Jill	Nursery	£12.00	40 sq.m	£480.00

EXERCISE 4

You will need to know how to:

▶ Use conditional formatting options

▶ Hide/unhide rows or columns

AM4.1.1 & AM4.1.2

1. Open the file *Selling*.

2. On the *furniture* worksheet, format the entries in the *Profit* column so that negative numbers show as bold, italic and green and figures between £0 and £50 show as bold, italic and purple.

3. Apply the same formatting to the **clothes** worksheet profits.

4. On this worksheet, hide the row displaying **Cowboy boots**.

5. Unhide the row.

6. Save and close the file.

4a – step 3

	A	B	C	D	E	F
1						
2	**ITEM**	**Bought**	**Sold**	**Profit**	**Place**	
3	Evening dress - patterned	£85.50	93.25	*£7.75*	Frock Exchange	
4	Day dress - linen stripes	£40	£35	*-£5.00*	Ebay	
5	Bow tie - velvet	£3.50	£28.99	*£25.49*	Local paper	
6	Day dress - cotton flowers	£15.55	£22.35	*£6.80*	Frock Exchange	
7	Cowboy boots	£100	£245	£145.00	Ebay	
8	Dressing gown	£24.99	£15.50	*-£9.49*	Local paper	
9						

4b – step 4

	A	B	C	D	E	F
1						
2	**ITEM**	**Bought**	**Sold**	**Profit**	**Place**	
3	Evening dress - patterned	£85.50	93.25	£7.75	Frock Exchange	
4	Day dress - linen stripes	£40	£35	-£5.00	Ebay	
5	Bow tie - velvet	£3.50	£28.99	£25.49	Local paper	
6	Day dress - cotton flowers	£15.55	£22.35	£6.80	Frock Exchange	
8	Dressing gown	£24.99	£15.50	-£9.49	Local paper	

EXERCISE 5

You will need to know how to:

◗ Use Paste Special options

◗ Link data within a worksheet

2

◊ECDL◊

AM4.1.1 & AM4.2.3

1. Open the workbook *Votes*

2. Add the row heading **TOTAL** in cell A10.

3. Total the votes cast for **Marion** in cell B10.

4. Total the votes for all other candidates.

5. Format the **TOTAL** row to bold with an outside border.

6. Enter **CANDIDATES** in cell A13 and **OVERALL VOTES** in cell B13.

7. Now copy the candidate names so they are transposed in cells A14:A18.

8. Next to the names, copy and transpose just the values of their total votes.

9. Reorder these entries so the candidates are displayed in descending order of total votes cast.

10. In cell A21 enter the following text: **The winner is Derek B with:**.

11. Copy his final total from cell B14 into cell B21, making sure you link the two cells.

12. Save your worksheet and print a copy.

13. Now change votes cast for Derek B by the Brighton branch to 107. Check that his overall vote in B14 and entry in cell B21 do *not* update.

14. Change the entry in cell B14 manually to 249. The entry in B21 should update automatically.

15. Save and close the file.

5 – step 12

	A	B	C	D	E	F
1	CANDIDATES VOTES					
2						
3	BRANCH	Marion	Derek K	Daniel	Sheila	Derek B
4	Loughborough	20	36	14	32	18
5	Leicester	44	59	38	22	66
6	Oxford	37	30	28	3	14
7	Brighton	79	45	62	78	93
8	Guildford	12	33	26	42	35
9	Newcastle	19	15	22	17	9
10	TOTAL	211	218	190	194	235
11						
12						
13	CANDIDATES	OVERALL VOTES				
14	Derek B	235				
15	Derek K	218				
16	Marion	211				
17	Sheila	194				
18	Daniel	190				
19						
20						
21	The winner is Derek B with:	235				
22						

EXERCISES 6 AND 7

You will need to know how to:

◗ Sort data by multiple columns

◗ Perform custom sorts

◗ Record a simple macro

◗ Run a macro

◗ Assign a macro to a custom button on the toolbar

 AM4.2.1 & AM4.5.1

Exercise 6   1. Start a new workbook.

2. Record a macro named **Centre** that will centre any data horizontally and vertically on the page.

3. Assign the macro to a custom button on the toolbar.

4. Open the workbook *Garden centre* and run the macro. Check in page preview that the macro has worked successfully.

5. Carry out a multiple sort on the plants: first by variety and then in descending order of the cost of one plant.

6. Re-order the plant varieties alphabetically and then in ascending order of final price.

7. Now carry out a custom sort so that the plants are in normal date order, i.e. all those sold in January, then February, then March, etc.

8. Save and close the file.

6a – step 5

	A	B	C	D	E	F
1	GARDEN CENTRE PLANTS					
2	DATE	VARIETY OF PLANT	COST OF 1 PLANT	COLOUR	NUMBER BOUGHT	FINAL PRICE
3	22-Jun	Crocus	£0.95	Purple	23	£21.85
4	05-Jun	Crocus	£0.95	Yellow	30	£28.50
5	14-May	Daffodil	£0.90	Yellow	60	£54.00
6	02-Jan	Dahlia	£2.50	Red and white	6	£15.00
7	08-Feb	Fritillary	£1.05	Purple	25	£26.25
8	17-Apr	Hyacinth	£2.35	Blue	18	£42.30
9	23-Mar	Lavender	£4.20	Pink	12	£50.40
10	06-Mar	Magnolia	£15.00	Pink	3	£45.00
11	05-Jun	Rose	£3.75	White	18	£67.50
12	01-May	Rose	£2.30	Red	14	£32.20
13	03-Feb	Tulip	£1.50	Yellow	9	£13.50

6b

Arial ▾ 10 ▾ **B** *I* <u>U</u> ≡ ≡ ≡ ▦ 🌐 % , ⁺.₀ .₀₀ ☺ ⇤ ⇥ ▦ ▾ ◌ ▾ **A** ▾ ▾

C21 ▾ *fx*   Centre

	A	B	C	D	E	F
1	GARDEN CENTRE PLANTS					
2	DATE	VARIETY OF PLANT	COST OF 1 PLANT	COLOUR	NUMBER BOUGHT	FINAL PRICE
3	02-Jan	Dahlia	£2.50	Red and white	6	£15.00
4	03-Feb	Tulip	£1.50	Yellow	9	£13.50
5	08-Feb	Fritillary	£1.05	Purple	25	£26.25
6	06-Mar	Magnolia	£15.00	Pink	3	£45.00
7	23-Mar	Lavender	£4.20	Pink	12	£50.40
8	17-Apr	Hyacinth	£2.35	Blue	18	£42.30
9	01-May	Rose	£2.30	Red	14	£32.20
10	14-May	Daffodil	£0.90	Yellow	60	£54.00
11	05-Jun	Rose	£3.75	White	18	£67.50
12	05-Jun	Crocus	£0.95	Yellow	30	£28.50
13	22-Jun	Crocus	£0.95	Purple	23	£21.85
14						

Exercise 7 1. Open *Courses*.

2. Carry out a sort to place courses in order of **Days** of the week and then by **Title** in ascending order.

3. Increase the morning Yoga class to £55.

4. Add three more courses:

Tuesday	2 – 5	French	LL2	£45
Thursday	2 – 4.30	German	LL4	£45
Monday	9 – 12	Cooking	12C	£75

5. Carry out a new sort: first by **Day** to keep the correct order of days in the week and then by **Cost** in descending order.

6. Check in print preview that there are no gridlines visible.

7. Record a macro that will set the page to landscape orientation and add gridlines. Name it **Landscape** and assign it to a button on the toolbar.

8. Copy the data to a new worksheet and run the macro.

9. Save and close the file.

7a – step 2

	A	B	C	D	E
1	Courses				
2	DAY	TIME	TITLE	ROOM	COST
3	Monday	2 - 5	Computing	12C	£60
4	Monday	9 - 12	Flower arranging	117A	£50
5	Tuesday	2 - 5	Yoga	14B	£45
6	Tuesday	9 - 12	Yoga	117A	£45
7	Wednesday	2 - 4.30	Dance	14B	£80
8	Thursday	9.30 - 12.30	Painting	122A	£105
9	Friday	9 - 12	Computing	122A	£60
10					

7b – step 4

	A	B	C	D	E
1	Courses				
2	DAY	TIME	TITLE	ROOM	COST
3	Monday	9 - 12	Cooking	12C	£75
4	Monday	2 - 5	Computing	12C	£60
5	Monday	9 - 12	Flower arranging	117A	£50
6	Tuesday	9 - 12	Yoga	117A	£55
7	Tuesday	2 - 5	French	LL2	£45
8	Tuesday	2 - 5	Yoga	14B	£45
9	Wednesday	2 - 4.30	Dance	14B	£80
10	Thursday	9.30 - 12.30	Painting	122A	£105
11	Thursday	2 - 4.30	German	LL4	£45
12	Friday	9 - 12	Computing	122A	£60

Courses

DAY	TIME	TITLE	ROOM	COST
Monday	9 - 12	Cooking	13C	£75
Monday	2 - 5	Computing	13C	£60
Monday	9 - 12	Flower arranging	117A	£50
Tuesday	9 - 12	Yoga	117A	£55
Tuesday	2 - 5	French	LL2	£45
Tuesday	2 - 5	Yoga	14B	£45
Wednesday	2 - 4.30	Dance	14B	£80
Thursday	9.30 - 12.30	Painting	122A	£105
Thursday	2 - 4.30	German	LL4	£45
Friday	9 - 12	Computing	122A	£60

EXERCISE 8

You will need to know how to:

▶ Hide/unhide worksheets

▶ Add or remove worksheet comments

▶ Edit worksheet comments

▶ Link data between worksheets

▶ Add a function to enter today's date

〈ECDL〉 **AM4.1.2, AM4.4.3, AM4.2.3 & AM4.3.1**

1. Open the *Expenses* workbook.

2. The *Own Car Mileage* sheet is hidden. Unhide the sheet.

3. On the *Own Car Mileage* sheet, add the following comment to cell C8: This will change in August to £0.45.

4. Edit the figure in the comment attached to cell F8 so that it reads: When this figure reaches 5000 please contact finance.

5. Remove the comment attached to cell E12 on the **Company Mileage** sheet that says: Total amount of miles for this journey.

6. On the *Claim Form* sheet, enter a formula in cell E33 that will display the total amount claimed by those using their own car.

7. On the same sheet, enter a formula in cell F33 to total the amount claimed by users of a company car.

8. Print a copy of the Claim Form worksheet only.

9. Now make the following changes:

    a. The book on Shakespeare costs £35.75.

    b. Company car mileage from Leicester to Truro was £280.

    c. Add an extra journey: David Wainright used his own car on 25 June to travel 62 miles from Bath to Swindon.

10. Print an updated copy of the *Claim Form* worksheet showing the new overall total.

11. Insert a new sheet named: *Journeys*.

12. Enter a function to add today's date to cell A1.

13. Hide this sheet.

14. Save and close the file.

8a – step 3

8b – step 7

	Arial	▾	12 ▾	**B**	*I*	<u>U</u>	≡	≡	≡	▦	🔲	%	,	+.0 .00	.00 +.0

| F33 | ▾ | *fx* ='Company Car Mileage'!F34 |

	A	B	C	D	E	F	G
2							
3				**NAME**		**David Wainright**	
4							
5				**ACCOUNT NUMBER**			
6							
7				**204459231**			
8							
9				**PERIOD OF CLAIM**		**Jun-06**	
10							
11							
12							
13							
14						**TRAVEL EXPENSES**	
					OWN Car Mileage	**COMPANY Car Mileage**	**Travel & Subsistence**
15		**DATE**	**DETAILS**	**TOTAL**			
16							
17	1	03/06/2006	Parking Birmingham conference	9.00			9.00
18	2	04/06/2006	Parking Birmingham conference	9.00			9.00
19	3	12/06/2006	Fuel hire car	13.13			
20	4	13/06/06	Shakespeare Today	24.50			
21	5			0.00			
22	6			0.00			
23	7			0.00			
24	8			0.00			
25	9			0.00			
26	10			0.00			
27	11			0.00			
28	12			0.00			
29	13			0.00			
30	14			0.00			
31	15			0.00			
32							
33			**Total Amount to be reimbursed**	158.23	66.00	36.60	18.00
34							
35							
36							
37							

8c – step 10

12			0.00
13			0.00
14			0.00
15			0.00
	Total Amount to be reimbursed		191.28

You will need to know how to:

♦ Import a text file

♦ Use sub-totalling features

◊ECDL◊ **AM4.1.1 & AM4.1.2**

Exercise 9 1. Start a new worksheet and import the text file *Dog show* that is delimited by tabs.

2. Format the column headings to bold and save the workbook as *Dogs*.

3. Re-order the data first by County and then by Entries in ascending order.

4. Use the subtotalling feature to total Entries at each change of County.

5. Hide the record rows and display only the subtotals.

6. Create new subtotals that count the number of Clubs at each change of County.

7. Display only the subtotals.

8. Save and close the file.

9a – step 4

		A	B	C	D	E
	1	CLUB	CLASS	COUNTY	WINNING OWNER	ENTRIES
	2	Stirling	Bulldog	Avon	Hardy	2
	3	Stirling	Terrier	Avon	Brown	3
	4	Stirling	Bulldog	Avon	Black	11
	5			**Avon Total**		16
	6	Big C	Labrador	Cumbria	Williams	8
	7	Big C	Greyhound	Cumbria	Harlow	10
	8			**Cumbria Total**		18
	9	Whetstone	Greyhound	Derbyshire	Matheson	7
	10	Whetstone	Spaniel	Derbyshire	Peters	15
	11	Whetstone	Boxer	Derbyshire	Dorling	15
	12			**Derbyshire Total**		37
	13	Furness	Boxer	Leicestershire	Stirt	7
	14	Stirling	Terrier	Leicestershire	Harris	16
	15			**Leicestershire Total**		23
	16	Hardy	Terrier	Oxfordshire	Sweet	6
	17	Big C	Spaniel	Oxfordshire	Makepeace	12
	18			**Oxfordshire Total**		18
	19	Dodge	Spaniel	Warwickshire	George	9
	20	Dodge	Bulldog	Warwickshire	Brown	12
	21			**Warwickshire Total**		21
	22			**Grand Total**		133

9b – step 5

1 2 3		A	B	C	D	E
	1	CLUB	CLASS	COUNTY	WINNING OWNER	ENTRIES
+	5			Avon Total		16
+	8			Cumbria Total		18
+	12			Derbyshire Total		37
+	15			Leicestershire Total		23
+	18			Oxfordshire Total		18
+	21			Warwickshire Total		21
-	22			Grand Total		133

9c

1 2 3		A	B	C	D	E
	1	CLUB	CLASS	COUNTY	WINNING OWNER	ENTRIES
+	5	3		Avon Count		
+	8	2		Cumbria Count		
+	12	3		Derbyshire Count		
+	15	2		Leicestershire Count		
+	18	2		Oxfordshire Count		
+	21	2		Warwickshire Count		
-	22	14		Grand Count		
	23					

Exercise 10

1. Start a new workbook and import the text file *Stationery*.

2. Save the spreadsheet as *Stationery2*.

3. Sort in ascending order of **Colour**.

4. Display the subtotals of **Price** for each **Colour**.

5. Now sort in descending order of **Item** and display subtotals for the number of each **Item**.

6. Remove the subtotals and save and close the file.

10a – step 4

	A	B	C	D	E
1	Item	Colour	Size	Price	Ordered
3		Cream Total		£4.50	
6		Green Total		£15	
8		Grey Total		£18.50	
11		Red Total		£15	
15		Silver Total		£45	
17		White Total		£3.99	
19		Yellow Total		£2.80	
20		Grand Total		£105.07	

10b – step 5

	Item		Colour	Size	Price	Ordered
Paper Count		2				
Mouse mat Count		2				
Mouse Count		2				
Folder Count		3				
Discs Count		2				
Grand Count		11				

EXERCISES 11 AND 12

You will need to know how to:

- Modify chart axes line width
- Format chart axes numbers or text
- Reposition chart elements
- Explode segments of a pie chart

[ECDL] **AM4.2.5**

Exercise 11
1. Open the file *Income* and display the line chart on the *Income 1* sheet.
2. Apply a thicker weight to the line.
3. Format the Y-axis numbers to show no decimals.
4. Format the names of the months along the X-axis to bold, font size 11.
5. Move the chart title to the top, right-hand corner.
6. Add a legend positioned at the bottom of the chart.
7. Format the X-axis line width so that it is a thicker line.
8. Now display the pie chart on the *Income 2* sheet.
9. Explode the segments of the chart.
10. Reposition the data labels if necessary so that they are all clearly visible.
11. Move the legend so that it is on the left of the chart.
12. Save these changes and close the file.

11a – step 6

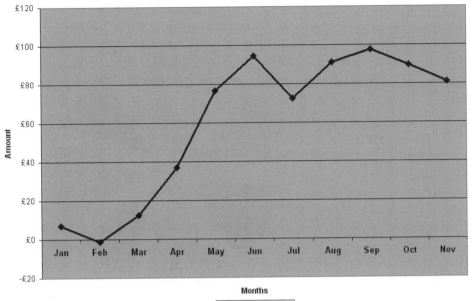

TOTAL INCOME

11b – step 7

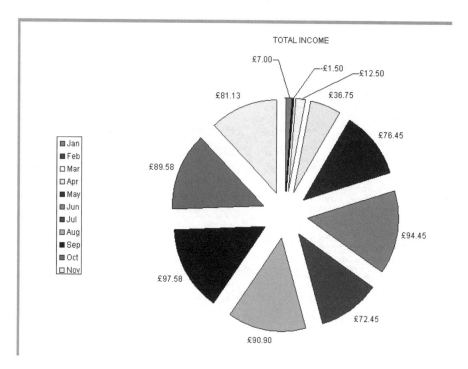

Exercise 12
1. Open *Decorating*.

2. Create an exploded pie chart showing the cost per sq. m of each type of curtain material.

3. Name the chart **Cost of Material** and add data labels showing the costs.

4. Move the chart title to the top, left-hand corner and increase the font to size 16.

5. Position the legend just below the title.

6. Drag out the sector of the chart showing the cheapest material.

7. Now create a column chart showing the final price for each room.

8. Reformat the Y-axis data to show currency with 0 decimal places.

9. Increase the line weight of both X and Y axes.

10. Format axes labels and values to Times New Roman bold.

11. Remove the legend.

12. Increase and emphasize the title font and move the title onto the plot area.

13. Save and close the file.

12a – step 6

Cost of Material

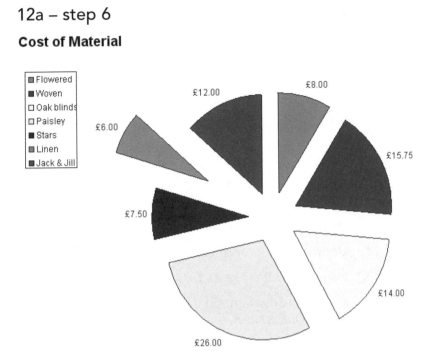

12b

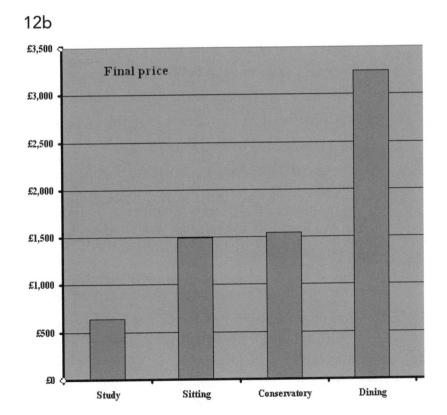

You will need to know how to:

- Protect/unprotect a worksheet with a password
- Protect/unprotect designated cells
- Use HLOOKUP and VLOOKUP functions

◊ECDL◊ **AM4.1.3 & AM4.3.1**

1. Open the workbook *Orders*.

2. Unprotect the worksheet *Discounts*. The password is **discount**.

3. Name the cell range A1:C6 as *discount*.

4. To find the discount on a cash order of £700, enter this figure in cell C2 on the *Orders* sheet.

5. Use the VLOOKUP function in C3 to find the discount.

6. Format the figure to percentage.

7. Work out the net value in C4.

8. Now find out the net value for a credit order of £850.

9. Format order and net value figures to currency with 0 decimal places.

10. Increase the credit order value to £1,100 and update the sheet.

11. Now name all the data on the *Warehouse* sheet as *material*.

12. On the *Orders* worksheet, type the words **Materials** in A13 and **Value** in B13.

13. In A14, enter the date **13 March 2006**.

14. Use the HLOOKUP function in B14 to find the exact value for plastic sold on that day.

15. Enter the date **5 April 2006** in cell A15 and use the HLOOKUP function in B15 to display the value for wood sold on that day.

16. Format the figures to currency.

17. Protect the *Warehouse* sheet using the password **warehouse**, but allow users to edit the entries in the **Wood** column cells.

18. Amend the entry for wood sold on 5 April to £65.50 and update the entries on the *Orders* sheet.

19. Save and close the workbook.

13a – step 10

	A	B	C
1	**CASH ORDER**		
2	Order Value		£700
3	Discount		10%
4	Net Value		£630
5			
6	**CREDIT ORDER**		
7	Order Value		£1,100
8	Discount		10%
9	Net Value		£990
10			

13b

Arial — 10 — **B** *I* U ≡ ≡ ≡ ⊞ 🈂 %

B14 ▾   *fx* =HLOOKUP("plastic",material,6,FALSE)

	A	B	C	D	E
11					
12					
13	MATERIALS	VALUE			
14	13-Mar	£34.45			
15	05-Apr	£65.50			

EXERCISE 14

You will need to know how to:

▶ Use logical functions

▶ Use nested functions

▶ Use text functions

▶ Create a pivot table

▶ Group data in a pivot table

▶ Modify the data source and refresh the pivot table

 AM4.3.1 & AM4.4.1

1. Open the workbook *Biscuits*.

2. Add a new column heading in G1: ORDERS UNDER £40.

3. Use an IF function in column G to display the text **Yes** if final totals are under £40 and **No** if final totals are £40 or more.

4. Apply conditional formatting so that all **Yes** entries are coloured red.

5. Head a new column **LOW ORDERS FROM FROSTS** and use a function to find out if there are any orders from Frosts which are below £40. If they are, display the word **low**, otherwise display the word **NOT**.

6. Use a text function to change all column headings to Title Case and format them in bold.

7. Create a pivot table on a new sheet that will sum the final totals for each company.

8. Format the figures to currency and apply your chosen Autoformat.

9. Now show the final totals for each order grouped by month.

10. Amend the pivot table to display the number of orders in each month.

11. Make the following changes to the data:

    a. The value of Plain wheat biscuits should be £45.50.

    b. Discount in July increased to 12%.

    c. The order on 6 July did not arrive so should be deleted.

12. Refresh the data in the pivot table and print a copy showing final totals before saving and closing the file.

14a – step 5

	H9		f_x =IF(AND(C9="Frosts",F9<40),"low","NOT")					
	A	B	C	D	E	F	G	H
1	DATE	VARIETY	COMPANY	VALUE	DISCOUNT	FINAL TOTAL	ORDERS UNDER £40	LOW ORDERS FROM FROSTS
2	02-Apr	Plain wheat	Macwhirtle	£42.00	5%	£39.90	Yes	NOT
3	13-Apr	Chocobiks	Spenders	£65.00	5%	£61.75	No	NOT
4	25-May	Orange sandwich	Macwhirtle	£28.50	5%	£27.08	Yes	NOT
5	30-May	Coffee cream	Frosts	£36.00	5%	£34.20	Yes	low
6	12-Jun	Pinwheel	Harding	£42.45	10%	£38.21	Yes	NOT
7	18-Jun	Wafers - raspberry	Spenders	£78.00	10%	£70.20	No	NOT
8	25-Jun	Whole wheat	Macwhirtle	£26.49	10%	£23.84	Yes	NOT
9	01-Jul	Meringue	Frosts	£35.00	10%	£31.50	Yes	low
10	06-Jul	Nut wafer	Frosts	£47.00	10%	£42.30	No	NOT
11	19-Jul	Wafers - blackcurrant	Spenders	£82.99	10%	£74.69	No	NOT
12								

14b – step 8

3	Company ▼	Final Total
4	Frosts	£108.00
5	Harding	£38.21
6	Macwhirtle	£90.82
7	Spenders	£206.64
8	**Grand Total**	**£443.66**

14c – step 9

3	Date	Final Total
4	Apr	£101.65
5	May	£61.28
6	Jun	£132.25
7	Jul	£148.49
8	Grand Total	£443.66

14d

3	Date	Final Total
4	Apr	£104.98
5	May	£61.28
6	Jun	£132.25
7	Jul	£103.83
8	Grand Total	£402.33

EXERCISE 15

2

You will need to know how to:

- ◗ Delete a data series in a chart
- ◗ Widen the gap between chart columns
- ◗ Insert an image into a 2D chart
- ◗ Modify the chart type for a defined data series

 AM4.2.5

1. Open the file *Villas* and create a 2D column chart showing bookings for all countries over the whole year. Make sure X-axis category labels display the names of the countries.

2. You want to see bookings without summer data. Remove the 3rd quarter data series from the chart.

3. Cyprus bookings are no longer being taken. Remove all details of villas in this country from the chart.

4. Widen the gap between chart columns to 250.

5. Add a chart title: Villa Bookings Out of Season, and axes titles: **Countries** and **Bookings**.

6. Add the image *Hols* as a chart background.

7. Save and print a copy of the chart.

8. Create a new 3D column chart showing bookings for all countries except Cyprus for all four quarters.

9. Modify the chart type for the 3rd quarter data series, e.g. select a cone or cylinder type.

10. Save and close the file.

15a – step 1

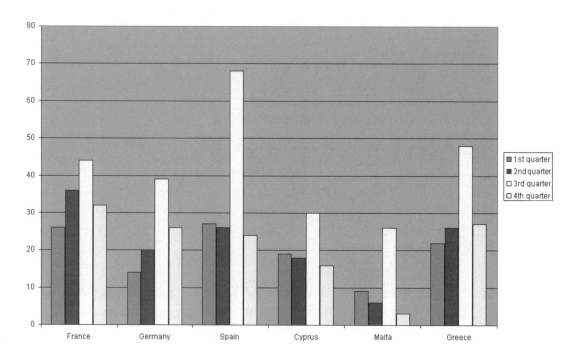

15b – step 4

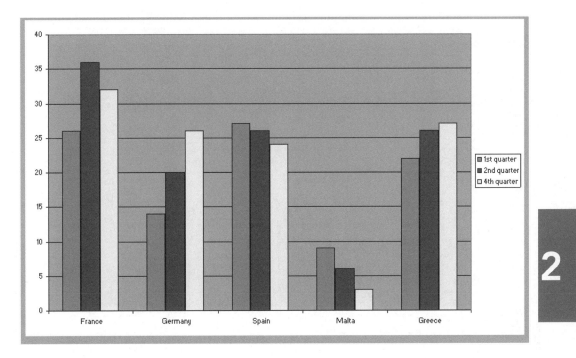

15c – step 6

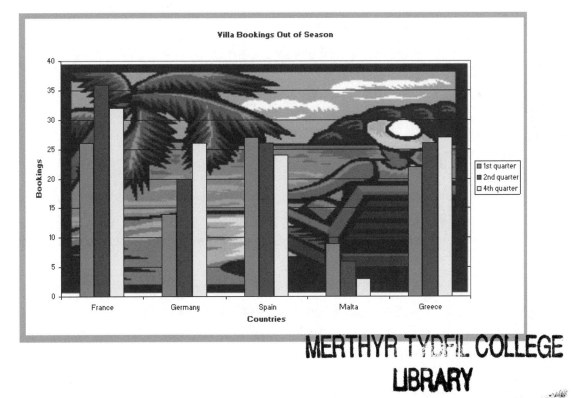

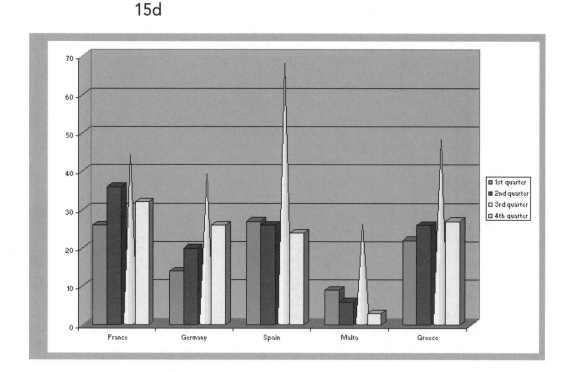

EXERCISE 16

You will need to know how to:

▶ Protect/unprotect a workbook

▶ Create queries

▶ Use advance query/filter options

 AM4.1.4 & AM4.2.2

1. Create a new workbook named *Jobs*. Rename Sheet 1 as *London Jobs*.

2. You are going to search for records that are stored in the Access database *Employment*. Create a query that will display all records meeting the following criteria:

   a. Town is **London**.

   b. Start date is between January and March 2005.

3. Display only the following fields in the order: Job Title, Company, Salary, Start Date, Contact and Town.

4. Sort the records in descending order of **Start Date**.

5. Print a copy of the records.

6. Edit the query so that the **Salary** and **Town** fields are not displayed.

7. Print a copy of the query.

8. Name a new worksheet *More than 2 vacancies*.

9. Create a new query that will find all the jobs with three or more vacancies that offer a salary over £18500. Only display the following fields: **Company**, **Job Title**, **Vacancy Number**, **Salary** and **Town** and sort the records in descending order of **Salary**.

10. Use the advanced filter option to display only those records where the salary is between £19500 and £40000.

11. Hide the *More than 2 vacancies* worksheet.

12. Password-protect the workbook using the password **vacancies** and then save and close the file.

13. Re-open the file, unhide the sheet and format the salaries to currency with two decimal places.

14. Create a new query to display all the records in the *Employment* database.

15. Use the advanced filter option to display only those records where the **Job Title** relates to sales and the **Town** is *not* Manchester.

16. Print a copy of the results.

17. Remove the workbook password protection.

18. Save and close the file.

16a – step 4

JOB TITLE	COMPANY	SALARY	START DATE	CONTACT	TOWN
MARKETING OFFICER	SETTLES	35000	15/03/2005 00:00	MARY PIERCE	LONDON
SALES ASSISTANT	HAYWARDS	14850	17/02/2005 00:00	AMANDA DOBBS	LONDON
PURCHASING ASSISTANT	WILFREDS	23000	02/02/2005 00:00	STEWART HAVERS	LONDON

16b – step 6

JOB TITLE	COMPANY	START DATE	CONTACT
MARKETING OFFICER	SETTLES	15/03/2005 00:00	MARY PIERCE
SALES ASSISTANT	HAYWARDS	17/02/2005 00:00	AMANDA DOBBS
PURCHASING ASSISTANT	WILFREDS	02/02/2005 00:00	STEWART HAVERS

16c – step 10

COMPANY	JOB TITLE	VACANCY NUMBER	SALARY	TOWN
GEORGE FASHIONS	SALES ASSISTANT	4	19900	LONDON
SPENDERS	SYSTEMS ANALYST	3	32500	BRADFORD

16d

COMPANY	JOB TITLE	SALARY	TOWN	VACANCY NUMBER	START DATE	CONTACT
HAYWARDS	SALES ASSISTANT	14850	LONDON	2	17/02/2005 00:00	AMANDA DOBBS
SCOTS	SALES ASSISTANT	15500	BIRMINGHAM	3	14/08/2005 00:00	DON MISKIT
GEORGE FASHIONS	SALES ASSISTANT	19900	LONDON	4	03/05/2005 00:00	HUSSEIN MASSAM
SPENDERS	IT SALES	44000	LONDON	2	08/04/2005 00:00	STAN BERKLEY

EXERCISE 17

You will need to know how to:

◗ Link data between workbooks

◗ Link data into a word processed document

◗ Use statistical functions

 AM4.2.3 & AM4.3.1

1. Open the workbook *Freelance*.

2. Select and copy the cell range A2:C7.

3. Open the Word document *My invoice*, click after the sentence ending **new book** and press Enter.

4. Paste in the cells so that you add a link to the worksheet and then save and close the document.

5. Back in the workbook, add the following data:

Work	Hours
Proofreading	4
Liaising with author	2
Checking 2nd draft	4
Writing introduction	3

6. Re-open *My invoice* and check that the total has updated.

7. Print a copy of the document and then save and close the *My invoice* file.

8. Now open the workbook *My earnings* and *link* just the total in *Freelance* to the freelance income for April on the *Earnings* worksheet.

9. In the workbook *Freelance*, increase the hours spent liaising with the author to six. Check in *Earnings* that the freelance earnings for April have been updated automatically.

10. Close the *Freelance* workbook.

11. In row 27 on the *Savings* worksheet of *My earnings*, use a function to display how many months showed a negative balance. Head the row **Negative balance**.

12. Some of the cells have text entries or are empty. In row 28, use a function to display the number of cells in the range B2:B26 that contain a value. Head the row **Contain a value**.

13. Finally, use a function in row 29 to display the number of cells in the range B2:B26 that are not blank. Head the row **Not empty**.

14. Save and close the file.

17a – step 6

23 Ardley Court
Hanwell
London EC1

Dear John

Please find below details of my work on the new book.

Date	Work	Hours
05 April 2006	Proofreading	4
18 April 2006	Liaising with author	2
22 April 2006	Checking 2nd draft	4
29 April 2006	Writing introduction	3
TOTAL	rate £15 p.h.	£195

I look forward to receiving the money in the near future.

Best wishes

Sajit

17b – step 9

| B6 | ▼ | f_x | =[Freelance.xls]Sheet1!$C$7 |

	A	B	C	D	E
1	**Income for the year**				
2	Month	*Freelance income*	*Bar Work*	*Security*	
3	Jan	£750	£1,150	£85	
4	Feb	£235	£1,245	£85	
5	Mar	£185	£2,257	£85	
6	Apr	255			
7	May				
8	Jun				
9	Jul				
10	Aug				
11	Sep				
12	Oct				
13	Nov				
14	Dec				
15	TOTAL	£1,425	£4,652	£255	

17c

| B28 | ▼ | f_x | =COUNT(B2:B26) |

	A	B	C
1	**Balance in Special Account**		
2	Date	Amount	
3	Jan-05	£34.00	
4	Feb-05	£163.00	
5	Mar-05	-£30.00	
6	Apr-05	£18.00	
7	May-05	£246.00	
8	Jun-05	£92.00	
9	Jul-05		
10	Aug-05	£143.00	
11	Sep-05	£260.00	
12	Oct-05	-£21.00	
13	Nov-05	-£14.00	
14	Dec-05	£15.00	
15	Jan-06	£48.00	
16	Feb-06	£75.00	
17	Mar-06	£32.00	
18	Apr-06	-£129.00	
19	May-06		
20	Jun-06	£19.00	
21	Jul-06	£27.00	
22	Aug-06	£32.00	
23	Sep-06	£18.00	
24	Oct-06	-£3.00	
25	Nov-06	£23.00	
26	Dec-06	-£49.00	
27	Negative balance	6	
28	Contain a value	22	
29	Not empty	23	

You will need to know how to:

♦ Use mathematical functions

♦ Display formulae

 AM4.3.1 & AM4.4.3

Exercise 18 1. Open the workbook *Art*.

2. Add a new column heading **ROUNDED UP** and use a function to display the totals to the nearest £10.

3. Display the underlying formulae.

4. Freeze the panes so that you can display the row headings and just the total and rounded up figures. Print a copy and then return to normal view and display all columns again.

5. Format the rounded up figures to currency with 0 decimal places.

6. Add a new row heading **Overall Income** and use a function to total all the entries in the **TOTAL** column.

7. Below this, enter a new row heading **Totals for large orders** and use a function to display the total for all orders over £50.

8. Add a new column heading **BEST ORDERS** and use a function to display the following text: if totals are under £20 – **low**, if under £50 – **fine**, if under £80 – **good**, other orders – **excellent**.

9. Apply conditional formatting to the totals: under £50 = blue; under £80 = yellow; over £80 = red.

10. Save and close the workbook.

18a – step 4

	A	F	G
1	DRAWING MATERIALS		
2	ITEM	TOTAL	ROUNDED UP
3	ACRYLIC TUBE	=D3-(D3*E3)	=ROUND(F3,-1)
4	WATERCOLOUR TUBE	=D4-(D4*E4)	=ROUND(F4,-1)
5	WATERCOLOUR PAN	=D5-(D5*E5)	=ROUND(F5,-1)
6	CALLIGRAPHY PEN	=D6-(D6*E6)	=ROUND(F6,-1)
7	TRACING PAPER	=D7-(D7*E7)	=ROUND(F7,-1)
8	SKETCH PENCIL PACK	=D8-(D8*E8)	=ROUND(F8,-1)
9	COLOURED PENCIL PACK	=D9-(D9*E9)	=ROUND(F9,-1)
10	BOXED ACRYLIC PAINTS	=D10-(D10*E10)	=ROUND(F10,-1)
11	CHINESE PAINTING SET	=D11-(D11*E11)	=ROUND(F11,-1)
12			

18b

	A	B	C	D	E	F	G	H
1	DRAWING MATERIALS							
2	ITEM	NUMBER SOLD	UNIT PRICE	SALES INCOME	DISCOUNT	TOTAL	ROUNDED UP	BEST ORDERS
3	ACRYLIC TUBE	9	£3.75	£33.8	5%	£32	£30	fine
4	WATERCOLOUR TUBE	19	£2.99	£56.8	5%	£54	£50	good
5	WATERCOLOUR PAN	14	£1.45	£20.3	2%	£20	£20	low
6	CALLIGRAPHY PEN	3	£8.50	£25.5	8%	£24	£20	fine
7	TRACING PAPER	11	£6.40	£70.4	10%	£63	£60	good
8	SKETCH PENCIL PACK	13	£9.99	£129.9	5%	£123	£120	excellent
9	COLOURED PENCIL PACK	18	£7.50	£135.0	5%	£128	£130	excellent
10	BOXED ACRYLIC PAINTS	3	£18.75	£56.3	10%	£51	£50	good
11	CHINESE PAINTING SET	6	£24.00	£144.0	10%	£130	£130	excellent
12	Overall Income					£624.73		
13	Totals for large orders					£549.18		

Exercise 19
1. Open *Stationery2*.

2. Insert a new column named **Price in ££** between **Price** and **Ordered**.

3. Use a function to round up prices to the nearest whole pound.

4. Enter 12% in cell A15. This is the discount offered.

5. Add a new column headed **Discount**.

6. Use a formula to multiply **Prices** by the discount, using cell addresses and not actual figures.

7. Display the formulae used.

8. Add a new heading in A13: **TOTAL ORDERS** and work out the total in the Price column.

9. On the next row, work out the total for all stock that is less than £15. Head the row **LOW VALUE ORDERS**.

10. Save and close the file.

19a – step 7

D	E	F	G
Price	Price in ££	Ordered	Discount
4.5	=ROUND(D2,0)	5 packs	=$A$15*D2
3.99	=ROUND(D3,0)	10 packs	=$A$15*D3
2.8	=ROUND(D4,0)	2	=$A$15*D4
2.8	=ROUND(D5,0)	12	=$A$15*D5
2.99	=ROUND(D6,0)	6	=$A$15*D6
10.5	=ROUND(D7,0)	4 boxes	=$A$15*D7
18.99	=ROUND(D8,0)	2 boxes	=$A$15*D8
16	=ROUND(D9,0)	6	=$A$15*D9
18.5	=ROUND(D10,0)	7	=$A$15*D10
12	=ROUND(D11,0)	1	=$A$15*D11
12	=ROUND(D12,0)	2	=$A$15*D12

19b

	A	B	C	D	E	F	G
				D14	▼	f_x =SUMIF(D2:D12,"<15")	
	A	B	C	D	E	F	G
1	Item	Colour	Size	Price	Price in ££	Ordered	Discount
2	Paper	Cream	A4	£4.50	£5.00	5 packs	£0.54
3	Paper	White	A4	£3.99	£4.00	10 packs	£0.48
4	Folder	Green	A4	£2.80	£3.00	2	£0.34
5	Folder	Yellow	A4	£2.80	£3.00	12	£0.34
6	Folder	Red	A5	£2.99	£3.00	6	£0.36
7	Discs	silver	CD-R	£10.50	£11.00	4 boxes	£1.26
8	Discs	silver	CD-RW	£18.99	£19.00	2 boxes	£2.28
9	Mouse	Silver	Small	£16	£16.00	6	£1.92
10	Mouse	Grey	Medium	£18.50	£19.00	7	£2.22
11	Mouse mat	Red	Small	£12	£12.00	1	£1.44
12	Mouse mat	Green	Small	£12	£12.00	2	£1.44
13	TOTAL ORDERS			£105.07			
14	LOW VALUE ORDERS			£51.58			
15	12%						

EXERCISE 20

You will need to know how to:

▶ Consolidate data in adjoining worksheets using a 3D sum function

▶ Create named scenarios from defined cell ranges

▶ Create a scenario summary

◊ECDL◊

AM4.2.3 & AM4.4.2

1. Open the *Training* workbook.

2. On the *totals* sheet, use a 3D sum function to consolidate the yearly totals for all the training courses.

3. Print a copy of the results.

4. Work out the Income for all the courses by multiplying the Charges by the Number of bookings and add a total at the bottom of the column.

5. You want to see what would happen to the training budget if you increased the cost of classes.

6. Create a scenario named 'original' so that you have a copy of the default entries.

7. Now create a scenario named 'Increase 1' where courses cost as follows:

Word processing – beginners	£35
Spreadsheet – beginners	£35
Powerpoint	£35
Communicating skills	£50
Interviewing	£75
MIS	£65

8. View the new scenario and print a copy of the results.

9. Create two more scenarios named 'Increase 2' and 'Increase 3' where courses are costed as follows:

	Increase 2	Increase 3
Word processing – beginners	£40	£45
Spreadsheet – beginners	£40	£45
Powerpoint	£40	£45
Communicating skills	£60	£65
Interviewing	£80	£90
MIS	£70	£75

10. Produce a summary sheet showing the effects of the various scenarios.

11. Save and close the file.

20a – step 2

	A	B
1	Bookings	Numbers
2	Word processing - beginners	100
3	Spreadsheet - beginners	158
4	Powerpoint	514
5	Communicating skills	135
6	Interviewing	283
7	MIS	1064
8	TOTAL	2254

20b – step 7

	A	B	C	D
1	Bookings	Numbers	Charges	Income
2	Word processing - beginners	100	£35	£3,500
3	Spreadsheet - beginners	158	£35	£5,530
4	Powerpoint	514	£35	£17,990
5	Communicating skills	135	£50	£6,750
6	Interviewing	283	£75	£21,225
7	MIS	1064	£65	£69,160
8	TOTAL	2254		£124,155

20c – step 10

Scenario Summary					
	Current Values:	original	Increase 1	Increase 2	Increase 3
Changing Cells:					
$C$2	£45	£30	£35	£40	£45
$C$3	£45	£30	£35	£40	£45
$C$4	£45	£30	£35	£40	£45
$C$5	£65	£45	£50	£60	£65
$C$6	£90	£60	£75	£80	£90
$C$7	£75	£55	£65	£70	£75
Result Cells:					
$D$8	£148,785	£104,735	£124,155	£136,100	£148,785

EXERCISE 21

You will need to know how to use:

♦ Date functions

♦ Database functions

〈ECDL〉 **AM4.3.1**

1. Open the workbook *Rent*.

2. In cell D4, use the MONTH function and the current date in A12 to work out how many months the tenants have been at **13 Wickam Close**.

3. Replicate this formula to work out months of residency for all tenants.

4. Calculate what rent should have been paid by all the tenants in the **Projected Income** column.

5. Finally, calculate the shortfall in rents over the year.

6. Save the data and print a copy.

7. Head row 9: **STILL OWE RENT** and use a function to count how many tenants have not paid the full amount of rent, i.e. showing a positive shortfall.

8. Name the cell range A3:G8 as *properties*.

9. Head a new row: **HIGHEST RENT** and use a database function to display the highest rent for the flats, using the name *properties* in the formula.

10. Change the rent for **The Priory** to £14,500 and check that this is now shown as the highest rent.

11. Save and close the file.

21a – step 5

| | D6 | ▼ | fx =MONTH($A$12)-MONTH(B6) | | | |

	A	B	C	D	E	F	G
1	ANNUAL RENTAL INCOME						
2							
3	Property	Start date	Rent per month	Months in property	Projected Income	Actual Income	Shortfall
4	13 Wickam Close	14/02/2005	£850.00	9	£7,650.00	£7,650	£0.00
5	22 Greenways	02/03/2005	£1,120.00	8	£8,960.00	£7,840	£1,120.00
6	4 The Oaks	18/03/2005	£685.00	8	£5,480.00	£5,480	£0.00
7	The Priory	24/01/2005	£990.00	10	£9,900.00	£8,650	£1,250.00
8	67 Sentinal Road	09/01/2005	£525.00	10	£5,250.00	£4,390	£860.00
9							
10							
11	Today's Date						
12	16/11/2005						

21b – step 7

| | G9 | ▼ | fx =COUNTIF(G4:G8,"<>0") | | | |

	A	B	C	D	E	F	G
1	ANNUAL RENTAL INCOME						
2							
3	Property	Start date	Rent per month	Months in property	Projected Income	Actual Income	Shortfall
4	13 Wickam Close	14/02/2005	£850.00	9	£7,650.00	£7,650	£0.00
5	22 Greenways	02/03/2005	£1,120.00	8	£8,960.00	£7,840	£1,120.00
6	4 The Oaks	18/03/2005	£685.00	8	£5,480.00	£5,480	£0.00
7	The Priory	24/01/2005	£990.00	10	£9,900.00	£8,650	£1,250.00
8	67 Sentinal Road	09/01/2005	£525.00	10	£5,250.00	£4,390	£860.00
9	STILL OWE RENT						3
10							
11	Today's Date						
12	16/11/2005						

21c – step 9

| | B10 | ▼ | fx =DMAX(properties,3,C4:C8) | | | |

	A	B	C	D	E	F	G
1	ANNUAL RENTAL INCOME						
2							
3	Property	Start date	Rent per month	Months in property	Projected Income	Actual Income	Shortfall
4	13 Wickam Close	14/02/2005	£850.00	9	£7,650.00	£7,650	£0.00
5	22 Greenways	02/03/2005	£1,120.00	8	£8,960.00	£7,840	£1,120.00
6	4 The Oaks	18/03/2005	£685.00	8	£5,480.00	£5,480	£0.00
7	The Priory	24/01/2005	£990.00	10	£9,900.00	£8,650	£1,250.00
8	67 Sentinal Road	09/01/2005	£525.00	10	£5,250.00	£4,390	£860.00
9	STILL OWE RENT						3
10	HIGHEST RENT	1120					

EXERCISES 22 AND 23

You will need to know how to:

▶ Use financial functions

Exercise 22 1. Open the file *Loan*.

2. Use the financial function PMT to work out how much your monthly payments will be if, as shown, you make a down payment of £5,000 for a car worth £18,500 and pay back the loan over four years at 4.9%.

3. You now find you can only put down £2,500. Change the down payment figure on your spreadsheet.

4. How many years will you need to pay off the loan if you keep payments to around £310 per month?

5. Save and close the file.

22a – step 2

	A	B
1	**Car Loan**	
2	Number of years to pay back loan	4
3	Total Number of payments	48
4	Loan Amount	£13,500
5	Interest Rate for Loan	4.90%
6	Down Payment	£5,000
7	MONTHLY PAYMENT	-£310.28
8		
9		
10	Cost of car	£18,500

22b

B7   *fx* =PMT(B5/12,B3,B4)

	A	B
1	**Car Loan**	
2	Number of years to pay back loan	4.85
3	Total Number of payments	58.2
4	Loan Amount	£16,000
5	Interest Rate for Loan	4.90%
6	Down Payment	£2,500
7	MONTHLY PAYMENT	-£309.43
8		
9		
10	Cost of car	£18,500

Exercise 23 1. Start a new workbook and save as *Annuity*.

2. Enter details of the following: an annuity you are considering buying will pay out £250 every month for the next 20 years. The cost of the annuity is £60,000 and the money paid out will earn 6%.

3. Use the PV function to find out what the annuity is worth today, i.e. if it is a good investment.

4. Save and close the file.

ANSWER 23

	B5	▾	f_x	=PV(B1/12,B4*12,-B2,0,0)	
	A		B	C	D
1	Rate		6%		
2	Monthly payments		£250		
3	Cost		£60,000		
4	Years		20		
5	Value		£34,895.19		

EXERCISE 24

You will need to know how to:

▶ Use 1-input data tables

▶ Trace precedent cells in a worksheet

▶ Trace dependent cells in a worksheet

 AM4.1.2 & AM4.4.3

1. Open the workbook *Savings*.

2. In cell B1, enter the interest rate 0.25%.

3. In cell C3, use the FV function to display the future value of £150 savings in an account paying 0.25% over two years.

4. In column B, enter the following range of interest rates: 0.25%, 0.5%, 0.75%, 1%, 1.25% and 1.5%.

5. Create a 1-input data table that will display the future value of your savings at the different interest rates.

6. Select cell C3 and use the trace precedent command to locate all cells referred to by the formula.

7. Open the *Expenses* workbook and use the trace dependent command to locate cells used in the formula in cell G33 on the *claim form* worksheet.

8. Select cell D33 and trace precedent cells.

9. Remove all arrows and then close both files.

24a – step 5

	A	B	C
1	Current Interest Rate	0.25%	
2			FV
3			£3,705.42
4	New Interest Rates	0.25%	£3,705.42
5		0.50%	£3,814.79
6		0.75%	£3,928.27
7		1.00%	£4,046.02
8		1.25%	£4,168.21
9		1.50%	£4,295.03

24b – step 6

	A	B	C	D
1	Current Interest Rate	0.25%		
2			FV	
3			£3,705.42	
4	New Interest Rates	0.25%	£3,705.42	
5		0.50%	£3,814.79	
6		0.75%	£3,928.27	
7		1.00%	£4,046.02	
8		1.25%	£4,168.21	
9		1.50%	£4,295.03	
10				

24c – step 7

Total Amount to be reimbursed	101.28	90.00	93.60	18.00

EXERCISE 25

You will need to know how to:

◗ Create a 2-input data table

 AM4.1.2

1. Open the *Mortgage* workbook.

2. In cell C3, use the PMT function to work out the repayments on a loan of £120,000 at the interest rate and term shown.

3. You want to find out what repayments would look like for the following interest rates: 4.25%, 4.5% and 4.75%, over a period of 10 or 15 years.

4. Add the interest rates in column C and the loan periods in row 3.

5. Create a 2-input table to display the results.

6. Print a copy and then save and close the file.

ANSWER 25

	A	B	C	D	E
1	Mortgage Repayments				
2			Current Repayments	10 years	15 years
3	Deposit	2,000	£791.95	120	180
4	Interest rate	5%	4.25%	£1,229.25	£902.73
5	Term (months)	240	4.50%	£1,243.66	£917.99
6	Loan	120000	4.75%	£1,258.17	£933.40

3

Module AM5: Database, Advanced Level

For this module you will need to understand relationships between tables and be able to design and edit tables; use a variety of query types; create and customize forms and reports; import and export data and perform calculations.

[Note: Copy the files from the CD onto your computer before you start. As they are read-only, you will not be able to make any changes if you open them directly from the disc.]

You will need to know how to:

- Apply and modify data types
- Create and edit a validation rule

AM5.1.1

1. Create a database file named *Sports*.

2. Design a table with the following field names and data types, leaving the properties as the default settings:

Field Name	Data Type
Item	Text
Size	Number
Price	Currency
Colour	Text
Order made	Date
Comments	Memo

3. Save the table as *Sports Goods* without a primary key and enter the following records:

Item	Size	Price	Colour	Order made	Comments
Shirt	30	£2.99	Blue	12/6/06	
Shorts	34	£3.75	Black	14/7/06	Send to the school
Shorts	30	£3.50	Black	18/7/06	
Shirt	28	£2.99	Blue	21/7/06	
Rugby shirt	32	£8.99	Red	21/7/06	May need to be changed as not sure of size
Shorts	32	£3.75	Blue	29/7/06	

4. Change the data type for *Order made,* e.g. to a medium or long date.

5. Change the data type for *Size* so that it will display decimals and then add a new record:

Item	Size	Price	Colour	Order made
Shirt	32.5	£2.99	Red	1 August 2006

6. Set up a validation rule that will only allow sizes between 26 and 36, and add relevant validation text.

7. Now try to enter the following record: **Shorts**, size **38** costing **£3.75** colour **Black** and **Order made on 3 August 2006**. Check that the rule works and change the size to 34.

8. Amend the validation rule and accompanying text to allow sizes up to 40.

9. Save the file.

1 – step 7

Item	Size	Price	Colour	Order made	Comments
Shirt	30	£2.99	Blue	12-Jun-06	
Shorts	34	£3.75	Black	14-Jul-06	Send to the sch
Shorts	30	£3.50	Black	18-Jul-06	
Shirt	28	£2.99	Blue	21-Jul-06	
Rugby shirt	32	£8.99	F		ed to be
Shorts	32	£3.75	B		
Shirt	32.5	£2.99	F		
Shorts	38	£0.00			
		£0.00			

Microsoft Access

⚠ Only sizes between 26 - 36

[OK]   [Help]

EXERCISES 2 AND 3

You will need to know how to:

◆ Create and edit a lookup field

◆ Apply and modify default values in a field

◆ Set a mandatory data field

 AM5.1.1

Exercise 2 1. Return to the design view of the *Sports goods* table and change the **Colour** field to a lookup field.

2. Type the following list: **Black, Blue, Red, Green**.

3. Return to the table and change the **Rugby shirt** to **Green**.

4. Edit the list by adding **Yellow**.

5. As you sell mainly **Shorts**, set this as the default entry for the **Item** field.

6. Add a new record: **Rugby shirt**, size **36**, price **£9.50**, colour **Yellow**, ordered on 4/8/06 with no comments.

7. Change the default **Item** entry to **Shirt**.

8. Make the **Size** field mandatory and try to create a new record without entering the size. You should see an error message.

9. Save and close the file.

2a – step 3

	Item	Size	Price	Colour	Order made	Comments
	Shirt	30	£2.99	Blue	12-Jun-06	
	Shorts	34	£3.75	Black	14-Jul-06	Send to the sc
	Shorts	30	£3.50	Black	18-Jul-06	
	Shirt	28	£2.99	Blue	21-Jul-06	
✎	Rugby shirt	32	£8.99	Green ▼	21-Jul-06	May need to b
	Shorts	32	£3.75	Black	29-Jul-06	
	Shirt	32.5	£2.99	Blue	01-Aug-06	
	Shorts	34	£3.75	Red	03-Aug-06	
			£0.00	Green		

2b – step 7

Sports goods : Table

Field Name	Data Type	
Item	Text	
Size	Number	
Price	Currency	
Colour	Text	
Order made	Date/Time	
Comments	Memo	

General | Lookup

Field Size	50
Format	
Input Mask	
Caption	
Default Value	"Shirt"
Validation Rule	
Validation Text	

3

2c – step 8

```
Microsoft Access                                                    _ □ ×
File  Edit  View  Insert  Format  Records  Tools  Window  Help
```

	Shirt	28	£2.99	Blue	21-Jul-06	
	Rugby shirt	32	£8.99	Green	21-Jul-06	May need to be
	Shorts	32	£3.75	Blue	29-Jul-06	
	Shirt	32.5	£2.99	Red	01-Aug-06	
	Shorts	34	£3.75	Black	03-Aug-06	
	Rugby shirt	36	£9.50	Yellow	04-Aug-06	
	Shirt					
*	Shirt					

Microsoft Access

⚠ The field 'Sports goods.Size' cannot contain a Null value because the Required property for this field is set to True. Enter a value in this field.

OK   Help

Exercise 3

1. Open the *Company* database.

2. In the **Products edited** table, change the data type for **Category** to a lookup field and enter the numbers 1–10.

3. Make the **Quantity per Unit** field mandatory.

4. Now add a new record: **Scottish Longbreads, category 3.**

5. Leave out **Quantity per Unit**. Continue entering: **Unit Price $9, 10 in stock, 20 on order, re-order level 20, not discontinued.**

6. When the error message is displayed, add **Quantity per Unit: 8 boxes x 8 pieces.**

7. In design view, modify the default setting for **Discontinued** so that it is **Yes**.

8. Change the **Category** lookup field so the numbers go from 0–9.

9. Save and close the database.

3a – step 6

Röd Kaviar	8	24 - 150 g jars	$15.00	1(
Longlife Tofu	7	5 kg pkg.	$10.00	
Rhönbräu Klosterbier	1	24 - 0.5 l bottles	$7.75	1:
Lakkalikööri	1	500 ml	$18.00	
Original Frankfurter grüne Soße	2	12 boxes	$13.00	
Scottish Longbreads	3	8 boxes x 8 pieces	$9.00	
	3		$0.00	
	4			
	5			
	6			
	7			
	8			
	9			
	10			

3b – step 8

General	Lookup	
Display Control	Combo Box	
Row Source Type	Value List	
Row Source	0;1;2;3;4;5;6;7;8;9|	▼
Bound Column	1	
Column Count	1	
Column Heads	No	
Column Widths	2.54cm	
List Rows	8	
List Width	2.54cm	
Limit To List	Yes	

EXERCISES 4 AND 5

You will need to know how to:

- Import files into a database
- Group information in a query
- Use functions in a query
- Use wildcards in a query
- Use arithmetic, logical expressions in a query

◊ECDL◊ **AM5.2.2 & AM5.5.6**

Exercise 4

1. Create a new database named *Orders*.

2. Import the data on the *orders* worksheet of the *Order data.xls* file to create a new table named *Order details*.

3. Make the **Order** field the primary key field.

4. Import the data on the *contacts* sheet to create a new table named *Contact details*.

5. Make the **Contact ID** field the primary key field.

6. You are going to create a query that shows the total sales for each item in the *Order details* table.

   a. Create a new field named **Totals** that multiplies the **Price** field by the **Number** field.

   b. Display only the **Gadget** and **Totals** fields.

   c. Group by **Gadget**.

d. Sum the Totals.

e. Name the query Total orders.

7. Create a new query and use a wildcard to find records in the *Contact details* table for all contacts who work for companies beginning with S.

   a. Display the First Name, Surname, Company and Position only.

   b. Save as S company contacts.

8. Amend the properties of the Surname field so that all text is displayed in upper case. Run the S company contacts query to check that the change has been applied.

9. Now create a new query that will display all records for gadgets that were delivered in March or May and are under £30.

   a. Display the Gadget, Price and Delivery fields only.

   b. Sort in descending order of Price.

   c. Save as Cheap March or May Goods.

10. Save and close the database file.

4a – step 6 (design view)

4b – step 6

Total orders : Select Query

Gadget	Totals
▶ Document holder	29.97
Keyboard	191.96
Manual	269.5
Monitor	315.98
Mouse	311.5

4c – step 8

S company contacts : Select Query

First name	Surname	Company	Position
Harold	DOWNE	Stantons	Deputy Manager
Pam	TERRY	Stacco	Purchasing Director

4d

Cheap March or May Goods : Select Query

Gadget	Price	Delivery
▶ Mouse	£24.50	22/05/2006
Manual	£24.50	16/05/2006
Manual	£24.50	22/05/2006
Mouse	£19.99	23/05/2006
Mouse	£16.50	02/03/2006
Document holder	£11.25	03/05/2006
Document holder	£9.99	14/03/2006

Exercise 5

1. Create a database named *Vegetables*.

2. Import the text file *Veg* to create a table named *Varieties*.

3. Create a query that will group the records by **Group** and count the number of **Varieties** in each group.

4. Change the name of the **Number in pack** field to **Number**.

5. Create a new query to display the price per seed of all varieties. Display the **Variety** and **Group** fields and format the **Seed price** to currency.

6. Save as *Price per seed*.

7. Edit the query to display only seed prices for varieties in a group containing the letter O.

8. Close the query without saving this change, and then close the database.

5a – step 3

Query1 : Select Query

Group	CountOfVariety
Brussels Sprout	2
Garlic	2
Onion	3
Potato	2

5b – step 6

Price per seed : Select Query

Variety	Group	Seed price
Bulldog	Onion	£0.04
Centurion	Onion	£0.04
Sturon	Onion	£0.04
Elephant	Garlic	£0.70
Giant Wight	Garlic	£1.98
Kerrs Pink	Potato	£0.22
Icarus F1	Brussels Sprout	£0.39
Cabbage Castello	Brussels Sprout	£0.41
Mimi	Potato	£0.18

5c – step 7

Price per seed : Select Query

Variety	Group	Seed price
Icarus F1	Brussels Sprout	£0.39
Cabbage Castello	Brussels Sprout	£0.41
Bulldog	Onion	£0.04
Centurion	Onion	£0.04
Sturon	Onion	£0.04
Kerrs Pink	Potato	£0.22
Mimi	Potato	£0.18

EXERCISE 6

You will need to know how to:

- Create and edit an input mask
- Create an update query
- Create a delete query

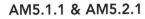

1. Open the *Friends* database and *My friends* table.

2. For the Telephone field, create an input mask that will ensure entry of the STD code as well as the main number e.g. 01357-445336.

3. Add the following record: Mary, mwhite@hotmail.com, 33 West Hall Street, 01457-993881, Haines, 14/5/87.

4. Edit the input mask so that the STD code is bracketed.

5. Add a further record: Jim, jimbo@yahoo.co.uk, 2 Melkin Road, (01457)-112332, Bennet, 2/2/88.

6. The name of the teacher in the Class field needs to be changed from Bennet to Bentley. Create and run an update query to do this.

7. Now create a query to delete all records for friends using a hotmail e-mail address.

8. Close the query and re-open the table to check that the records have been deleted.

9. Save and close the file.

6a – step 3

My friends : Table

Nickname	e-mail	Road	Telephone	Class	Birthday
Harry	hspens@hotmail.com	12 Walker Street	01297-334551	Jacko	27/09/1988
Pete	peterb@yahoo.co.uk	9 Stanley Close	01297-498221	Bennet	14/03/1989
Star	sarahp127@btinternet.com	84 Clarendon House	01457-239560	Small	02/06/1988
Geordie	bghope@virgin.net	17 Walker Street	01297-498768	Jacko	06/06/1989
Mary	mwhite@hotmail.com	33 West Hall Street	01457-993881	Haines	14/05/1987

6b – step 5

My friends : Table

Nickname	e-mail	Road	Telephone	Class	Birthday
Harry	hspens@hotmail.com	12 Walker Street	(01297)-334551	Jacko	27/09/1988
Pete	peterb@yahoo.co.uk	9 Stanley Close	(01297)-498221	Bennet	14/03/1989
Star	sarahp127@btinternet.com	84 Clarendon House	(01457)-239560	Small	02/06/1988
Geordie	bghope@virgin.net	17 Walker Street	(01297)-498768	Jacko	06/06/1989
Mary	mwhite@hotmail.com	33 West Hall Street	(01457)-993881	Haines	14/05/1987
Jim	jimbo@yahoo.co.uk	2 Melkin Road	(01457)-112332	Bennet	02/02/1988

6c – step 6

Query1 : Update Query

My friends

e-mail
Road
Telephone
Class
Birthday

Field:	Class
Table:	My friends
Update To:	"Bentley"
Criteria:	"Bennet"
or:	

6d – step 7

My friends : Table

Nickname	e-mail	Road	Telephone	Class	Birthday
#Deleted	#Deleted	#Deleted	#Deleted	#Deleted	#Deleted
Pete	peterb@yahoo.co.uk	9 Stanley Close	(01297)-498221	Bentley	14/03/1989
Star	sarahp127@btinternet.com	84 Clarendon House	(01457)-239560	Small	02/06/1988
Geordie	bghope@virgin.net	17 Walker Street	(01297)-498768	Jacko	06/06/1989
#Deleted	#Deleted	#Deleted	#Deleted	#Deleted	#Deleted
Jim	jimbo@yahoo.co.uk	2 Melkin Road	(01457)-112332	Bentley	02/02/1988

EXERCISES 7 AND 8

You will need to know how to:

▶ Create a parameter query

▶ Use a make table query to save information as a table

 AM5.2.1 & AM5.2.3

Exercise 7

1. Open the *Holiday* database.

2. Create a parameter query displaying all fields that will require the name of the Country before it can be run.

3. Run the query to find all hotels in Cyprus with 55 or more bedrooms.

4. Save as *Large hotels* and then close the query.

5. Use the query to find any large hotels in Spain.

6. Now create a query to save all Cyprus hotel records into a new table. Name the table *Cyprus hotels*.

7. Close the file.

7a – step 3

	Name	Country	Bedrooms	Swimming Pool	Miles from airport
	San Moreno	Cyprus	150	☑	50
	Serino	Cyprus	55	☐	65

7b – step 5

📄	Create query in Design view	
📄	Create query by using wizard	
🖾	Large hotels	

Enter Parameter Value ✕

enter country

Spain|

OK   Cancel

7c

Cyprus hotels : Table   _ □ ✕

	Name	Country	Bedrooms	Swimming Pool	Miles from airport
▶	San Moreno	Cyprus	150	☑	50
	Serino	Cyprus	55	☐	65
	Coral	Cyprus	24	☐	75

Record: ◄◄ ◄ [1] ► ►► ►✳ of 3

Exercise 8

1. Open the *Vegetables* database created for Exercise 5.

2. Create a query to display all **Variety** packs costing £4.50 or more, where you need to enter the name of the **Group** before it can be run.

3. Format the **Price** field to currency.

4. Search for potatoes meeting the criteria and save the query as *Expensive varieties*.

5. Create a query that will save records showing full details of all varieties dispatched in December or January to a new table named *Winter delivery*.

6. In the design of the table, format the **Price** field to currency.

7. Save the query as *Winter dispatch*.

8. In design view, set the primary key in the *Varieties* table as **Code** and set it as a text data type.

9. Save and close the database.

8a – step 4

Expensive varieties : Select Query

Variety	Group	Price
Kerrs Pink	Potato	£6.54
Mimi	Potato	£4.50

8b – step 7

Winter delivery : Table

Variety	Group	Dispatch	Code	Number	Price
Bulldog	Onion	December	11073	75	£2.95
Centurion	Onion	December	11076	75	£2.75
Sturon	Onion	December	11077	75	£2.75
Giant Wight	Garlic	December	11089	2	£3.95
Kerrs Pink	Potato	December	11214	30	£6.54
Mimi	Potato	January	11324	25	£4.50

EXERCISE 9

You will need to know how to:

- Create a crosstab query
- Create an append query
- Export data

AM5.2.1, AM5.2.2 & AM5.6.1

1. In the *Orders* database, create a crosstab query that will display the total Price of all the Gadgets by Make. The types of gadget should be shown as column headings.

2. Format the properties of the Totals field to currency.

3. Save the query as *Crosstab*.

4. Now edit the query so that you display the minimum value of each order, but do not save this change.

5. Import the new orders from the file *New orders.xls* to add them to the *Order details* table.

6. Run the crosstab query to display totals by type of gadget for all the orders now in the table.

7. Use a make table query to create a new table called *Manual orders* that will contain all orders for manuals.

8. Now create an append query that will add all document holder orders to the table.

9. Rename the table *Manuals and document holders*.

10. Export the records in the *Order details* table, including the field names, to a delimited text file.

11. Save the file as *Order details text*.

12. Close all open files.

9a – step 2

Make	Document holder	Keyboard	Manual	Monitor	Mouse
Brit publications			£269.50		
Pinco					£115.50
Pritts	£29.97				
Welstead		£191.96		£315.98	
Xana					£196.00

Query1 : Crosstab Query

9b – step 4

Query1 : Crosstab Query

Order Details
Gadget
Make
Price
Number
Delivery

Field:	Make	Gadget	Totals: [price]*[number]
Table:	Order Details	Order Details	
Total:	Group By	Group By	Min
Crosstab:	Row Heading	Column Heading	Value
Sort:			
Criteria:			
or:			

9c – step 6

crosstab : Crosstab Query

Make	Document holder	Keyboard	Manual	Monitor	Mouse
Brit publications			£344.50		
Drakes					£74.10
Pinco					£350.42
Pritts	£29.97			£398.00	
Stays				£336.99	£79.96
Treehouse books			£204.50		
Welstead	£168.75	£371.94		£1,595.98	
Xana		£401.50			£330.00

3

9d – step 9

Manuals and document holders : Table

Gadget	Make	Price	Number	Delivery	Contact ID	Order
Manual	Brit publications	£24.50	8	22/05/2006	PV1	3
Manual	Brit publications	£24.50	3	16/05/2006	AS12	6
Manual	Treehouse books	£33.50	5	18/11/2006	RS12	14
Manual	Brit publications	£25.00	3	01/01/2007	AS12	19
Manual	Treehouse books	£18.50	2	18/09/2006	PV1	22
Document holder	Pritts	£9.99	3	14/03/2006	RS12	8
Document holder	Welstead		1	12/05/2006	PV1	11
Document holder	Welstead	£11.25	15	03/05/2006	CD4	15

9e – step 11

Order Details text - Notepad

File Edit Format View Help

```
Gadget,Make,Price,Number,Delivery,Contact ID,Order
Mouse,Pinco,£16.50,1.00,2/3/2006 00:00:00,AS12,1.00
Monitor,Welstead,£157.99,2.00,13/3/2006 00:00:00,DL7,2.00
Manual,Brit publications,£24.50,8.00,22/5/2006 00:00:00,PV1,3.00
Mouse,Pinco,£16.50,6.00,14/4/2006 00:00:00,AS12,4.00
Keyboard,Welstead,£47.99,4.00,2/5/2006 00:00:00,CD4,5.00
Manual,Brit publications,£24.50,3.00,16/5/2006 00:00:00,AS12,6.00
Mouse,Xana,£24.50,8.00,22/5/2006 00:00:00,CD4,7.00
Document holder,Pritts,£9.99,3.00,14/3/2006 00:00:00,RS12,8.00
Monitor,Welstead,£127.50,2.00,3/7/2006 00:00:00,CD4,9.00
Mouse,Pinco,£25.00,3.00,14/9/2006 00:00:00,AS12,10.00
Document holder,Welstead,,1.00,12/5/2006 00:00:00,PV1,11.00
Mouse,Xana,£33.50,4.00,14/6/2006 00:00:00,PV1,12.00
Monitor,Pritts,£199.00,2.00,2/9/2006 00:00:00,AS12,13.00
Manual,Treehouse books,£33.50,5.00,18/11/2006 00:00:00,RS12,14.00
Document holder,Welstead,£11.25,15.00,3/5/2006 00:00:00,CD4,15.00
Mouse,Stays,£19.99,4.00,13/9/2006 00:00:00,PV1,16.00
Keyboard,Welstead,£89.99,2.00,2/4/2006 00:00:00,RS12,17.00
Mouse,Drakes,£12.35,6.00,14/10/2006 00:00:00,RS12,18.00
Manual,Brit publications,£25.00,3.00,1/1/2007 00:00:00,AS12,19.00
Monitor,Welstead,£205.00,5.00,2/9/2006 00:00:00,RS12,20.00
Mouse,Pinco,£19.99,8.00,23/5/2006 00:00:00,RS12,21.00
Manual,Treehouse books,£18.50,2.00,18/9/2006 00:00:00,PV1,22.00
Keyboard,Xana,£199.00,1.00,8/6/2006 00:00:00,PV1,23.00
Monitor,Stays,£336.99,1.00,5/9/2006 00:00:00,AS12,24.00
Keyboard,Xana,£67.50,3.00,30/11/2006 00:00:00,CD4,25.00
```

EXERCISES 10 AND 11

You will need to know how to:

▶ Create a one-to-many relationship between tables

▶ Apply and use referential integrity

▶ Relate/join data when designing queries

▶ Apply automatic deletion of related records

▶ Refine queries using Null and NOT values

AM5.1.2 & AM5.2.3

Exercise 10 1. Open the database *Selling*.

2. Link the two tables using the **Customer** field, leaving the default settings.

3. Enforce referential integrity and select **Cascade Deleted Related Records**.

4. Save the relationship.

5. Open the Auctioned table and try to add the following record: Wardrobe, £86, WR1, JP8, 24/8/06.

6. When you see the error message, close the table.

7. Enter the following details into the Customers table: Probyn, Mrs, JP8, Birmingham, Collecting, used Paypal.

8. Reopen Auctioned and now add the new record for the sale of a wardrobe.

9. Delete the record for **Mr Bray** in the Customers table and check that the record for his purchase of **Scales** is deleted from the Auctioned table automatically.

10. Use a query to find out the details of any customers who have *not* paid for their purchase. Display the Title, Surname, Item, Price, Auction date and whether Collecting.

11. Refine the same query so that the **Paid** field has no criteria and you display only customers who are not male.

12. Save as *Female customers*.

13. Close the database.

10a – step 3

10b – step 9 (Scales deleted)

Auctioned : Table

Item	Price	Auction date	Code	Placed	Customer	Paid
Tray	£9.99	01/07/2006	TB1	1	XQ3	02/07/2006
Tray	£11.45	01/07/2006	TB2	2	VJ7	03/07/2006
Lamp	£4.99	07/07/2006	LP7	4	PR2	
Painting set	£18.50	07/07/2006	PS5	5	BL6	09/07/2006
Chair	£45.00	18/08/2006	CH8	7	FD5	20/08/2006
Chest of drawers	£55.99	18/08/2006	CD1	8	PP4	22/08/2006
Wardrobe	£86.00	22/08/2006	WR1	10	JP8	24/08/2006

10c – step 10

Query1 : Select Query

Title	Surname	Item	Price	Auction date	Collecting
Mr	Roberts	Lamp	£4.99	07/07/2006	☑

10d – step 12

Microsoft Access - [Female customers : Select Query]

File   Edit   View   Insert   Format   Records   Tools   Window   Help

Title	Surname	Item	Price	Auction date	Collecting
Mrs	Jennings	Tray	£11.45	01/07/2006	☐
Ms	Lemmon	Painting set	£18.50	07/07/2006	☐
Mrs	Peters	Chest of drawers	£55.99	18/08/2006	☐
Mrs	Probyn	Wardrobe	£86.00	22/08/2006	☑
*					

Exercise 11

1. Open the *Vegetables* database.

2. Create a new table named *Veg orders* by importing the same named spreadsheet file.

3. Set the primary key as the **Order number** field and leave the properties at their default settings.

4. Create a one-to-many relationship between the two tables using the **Code** field.

5. Try to enforce referential integrity. It should not be possible, so delete the link.

6. Make appropriate changes to the fields to allow you to link the tables and enforce referential integrity.

7. You want to delete the **Cabbage Castello** from your catalogue. Edit the relationship between the tables to delete orders for this variety automatically in the *Veg orders* table.

8. Now create a query that will remove all records related to the **Cabbage Castello Brussels** sprout from the *Varieties* table and check that orders 4 and 8 in the *Veg orders* table have been deleted as well.

9. Create a new query that will display all varieties that are not dispatched in December. Display **Variety**, **Group**, **Dispatch** and **Price**, and format the **Price** to currency.

10. Save as *Not December*.

11. Close the database.

11a – step 6

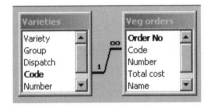

11b – step 8

Order No	Code	Number	Total cost	Name	Contact email
1	11237	5	9.75	Black	eb@virgin.net
2	11076	10	27.5	Black	eb@virgin.net
3	11087	7	48.65	Gordon	gordon@btinternet.com
5	11214	11	71.94	Hepple	hep23@compuserve.com
6	11073	7	20.65	Smythe	sm56@hardy.co.uk
7	11077	12	33	Rackham	rk_p@stanley.com
9	11089	3	11.85	Lindsey	lindseyx@orange.co.uk
10	11214	9	58.86	Whiteless	whiteless@compuserve.com

11c – step 10

Variety	Group	Dispatch	Price
Icarus F1	Brussels Sprout	May	£1.95
Elephant	Garlic	October	£6.95
Mimi	Potato	January	£4.50

You will need to know how to:

◆ Create bound and unbound controls on a form

◆ Create and edit a list box on a form

◆ Set sequential order of controls on a form

 AM5.3.1

Exercise 12 1. Open the *Holiday* database.

2. Create a form based on all the fields in the *Hotels* table.

3. Create a list box to offer a list of countries. The list should contain the following countries: Spain, Cyprus, France, Italy and Greece.

4. Use the form to add another hotel: the Giorgio in Italy has 200 bedrooms and a swimming pool and is 30 miles from the airport.

5. Add a label to the form header and enter the text: Hotel Entry Form.

6. Now add Malta to the list of countries in the list box.

7. Add a concatenated unbound text box in the form footer that will display both the Country and Bedrooms. Format in bold.

8. Finally, when entering data, it is found that hotel entries are listed first by country. Set the tab order to start with Country and then Miles from the airport before continuing with the default order.

9. Save and close the database.

12a – step 3

List Box Wizard

What values do you want to see in your list box? Enter the number of columns you want in the list, and then type the values you want in each cell.

To adjust the width of a column, drag its right edge to the width you want, or double-click the right edge of the column heading to get the best fit.

Number of columns: 1

	Col1
	Spain
	Cyprus
	France
	Italy
🖉	Greece
✱	

Cancel | < Back | Next > | Finish

12b – step 6

Hotels _ □ ×

Hotel Entry Form

▶ **Name**

Country | Malta

Bedrooms | 0

Swimming Pool ▨

Miles from airport | 0

Record: |◀ ◀ | 10 | ▶ ▶| ▶* | of 10

12c – step 7

Hotels _ □ ×

Hotel Entry Form

▶ **Name** | San Moreno

Country | France

Bedrooms | 150

Swimming Pool ☑

Miles from airport | 50

France 150

Record: |◀ ◀ | 1 | ▶ ▶| ▶* | of 9

12d – step 8

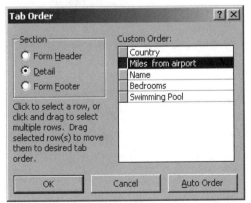

Tab Order ? ×

┌─ Section ────────────
○ Form Header
◉ Detail
○ Form Footer

Custom Order:

| Country |
| Miles from airport |
| Name |
| Bedrooms |
| Swimming Pool |

Click to select a row, or
click and drag to select
multiple rows. Drag
selected row(s) to move
them to desired tab
order.

OK | Cancel | Auto Order

1. Open the *Vegetables* database.

2. Create a form displaying all fields in the *Varieties* table.

3. Add an unbound textbox that concatenates **Group** and **Code**. Format the entry in red.

4. Replace the **Group** field with a list box offering a choice of all the groups currently showing in the table.

5. Return to the form.

6. Now edit the list to add **Leeks** and **Spinach**.

7. Use the form to add a new record: **Longbow Leek**, dispatched in **May**, code **11138**, and price **£5.95** for **60** plants.

8. Add the label: **Order Form** at the top of the form.

9. Change the tab order so that the form always starts with the **Group** field.

10. Save and close the database.

13a – step 3

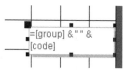

13b – step 6

Variety	Longbow

Group

	Potato
	Garlic
	Brussels spr
	Leeks
	Spinach

Dispatch	May

Code	11138

Number	60

Price	5.95

Leeks 11138

13c

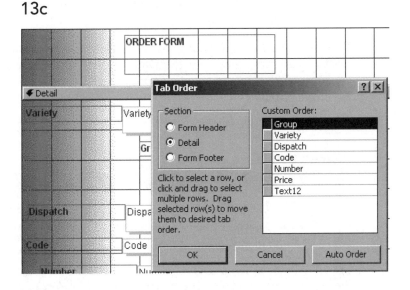

EXERCISES 14 AND 15

You will need to know how to:

- ♦ Create and edit combo boxes on a form
- ♦ Create check boxes on a form
- ♦ Create option groups on a form
- ♦ Create arithmetic, logical expression controls on a form

AM5.3.1

Exercise 14 1. Open the database *Music centre*.

2. Create a form named *Students* based on the *Students* table.

3. Create a combo box for **Class ID** entry that contains the instrument and the code. Label the instruction **Select instrument**.

4. Use the form to add another student record: Emma Wood, born 21/1/87, Female, lives at 36 Blue Brook, paid for lesson 3/4/06, hires an instrument, paid for the hire on 3/9/06 and is with teacher ME1. She plays violin and has the Student ID 011.

5. Replace the **Male** or **Female** control with an option group that is labelled **Gender**. Set the default as **Male**.

6. Add a checkbox labelled **Paid hire** that will show whether a student has paid the hire fee or not.

7. Close the form and add a new field to the *Students* table: **Today**. Enter the date 12/12/2006 into all records.

8. Return to the form and add a new calculated control labelled **Age**, based on the difference between the **Date of birth** and **Today** fields, with the result displayed in years. Set the properties to show only integer format, i.e. no decimals.

9. Save and close the form.

14a – step 5

14b – step 6

14c – step 8

Exercise 15 1. Open the *Jobs* database.

2. Create a form displaying all the fields.

3. Add a combo box so that users can select a contact's name and this will add the code automatically. Add the label Select contact for the code.

4. Edit the list to add a new contact: Jean, JS9.

5. Now add a control that will calculate the hourly rate (Salary divided by 52 and then by Hours). Label it: Hourly rate.

6. Close the form and add a new field to the table: Part time that displays the text Yes or No. Set it at Yes for all jobs over 35 hours.

7. Re-open the form and add an options group that will offer the choice of Location: Birmingham, Manchester, Bradford or Leeds. Set the default as Manchester.

8. Finally, add a check box that will be on for full time work and off for part time work. Label it Full time work.

9. Save and close the database.

15a – step 4

Job details

Job code	RM5
Interview room	C11
Title	Clerical officer
Salary	£12,500
Start date	22/08/2006
Location	Birmingham
Hours	18
Interview	12/06/2006
Contact name	Reg

Select contact for the code   Reg ▼

Contact ID:

George	GH7
Ken	KJ3
Mary	MS2
Larry	LM4
Reg	**RB5**
Jean	JS9

15b – step 5

Hourly rate	=[salary]/52/[hours]

15c – step 7

Location
- ⦿ Manchester
- ○ Leeds
- ○ Bradford
- ○ Birmingham

15d – step 8

⦿ Full time work

EXERCISE 16

You will need to know how to:

- ▸ Insert data fields into form headers or footers
- ▸ Create and modify subforms

1. Open the *Music centre* database.

2. Create a columnar form based on the *Classes* table.

3. Add a combo box in the form header that will allow users to go to a record by choosing an instrument from the list.

4. You need to create a *Payments* subform: first link the *Students* and *Classes* tables.

5. Now create the form by adding Instrument, Cost of class and Cost of hire from the *Classes* table, and Student ID, First name, Surname, Date class paid, Hires and Date hire cost paid from the *Students* table.

6. Display all violin students.

7. Now amend the subform so that it includes Date of birth and only displays records for students who hire instruments.

8. Check that there is only one record for students who play the recorder.

9. Save and close the database.

16a – step 3

16b – step 6

Payments

Instrument: Violin
Class per term (£): 100
Hire per term (£): 18
Student data

	First name	Surname	Date paid for lesson	Hires instrument	Date hire charge paid
▶	Paul	Wind	29/12/2006	☑	02/02/2006
	Nigel	Roach	02/01/2006	☑	14/02/2006
	Shirley	Black	02/01/2006	☑	15/03/2006
	Emma	Wood	03/04/2006	☑	03/09/2006
*				▨	

Record: 1 of 4

Record: 6 of 6

16c – step 7

Instrument: Violin
Class per term (£): 100
Hire per term (£): 18
Students subform1

	First name	Surname	Date of birth	Date paid for lesson	Hires instrument	Date hire charge paid
▶	Paul	Wind	01/04/1988	29/12/2006	☑	02/02/2006
	Nigel	Roach	02/01/1998	02/01/2006	☑	14/02/2006
	Shirley	Black	12/12/1987	02/01/2006	☑	15/03/2006
	Emma	Wood	21/01/1987	03/04/2006	☑	03/09/2006
*					▨	

Record: 1 of 4

16d

Payments

Instrument: Recorder
Class per term (£): 60
Hire per term (£): 5
Students

	First name	Surname	Date of birth	Date paid for less	Hires instrument	Date hire
▶	Diana	Golden	29/05/1998	13/02/2006	☑	
*					▨	

Record: 1 of 1

Exercise 17
1. Open the *Vegetables* database.

2. Create a subform for ordering that will display the following fields: **Group**, **Variety**, **Code** and **Price** (*Varieties* table) and **Number**, **Name** and **Contact email** (*Veg orders* table).

3. Edit the subform so that you only display records where the **Number** of vegetables ordered is fewer than 10.

4. Check that the record for Hepple is no longer shown.

5. Add a data field in the form header that will display the price after it is increased by 15% (i.e. multiplied by 1.15). The label should read: New price – plus 15%.

6. Format this price to currency.

7. Save and close the database.

17a – step 2

17b – step 3 – using Query Builder

17c

New price - plus 15% :

£7.52

Group	Potato
Variety	Kerrs Pink
Code	11214
Price	6.54

Veg orders

EXERCISES 18 AND 19

You will need to know how to:

▸ Create calculated controls in a report

▸ Calculate percentages in a report

▸ Use formulae in a report

◊ECDL◊ **AM5.4.1**

Exercise 18 1. Open the *Orders* database.

2. Create a report based on **Order details** grouped by **Make** that shows all the **Gadget** details except **Contact ID** and **Order**.

3. Sort in descending order of **Price**.

4. Display the average number of orders for each **Gadget** and label this entry **Average order**.

5. Format this in bold, with no decimal places.

6. Now delete the averages and add a control that will calculate the total value of orders for each company, based on multiplying **Price** by **Number** and then totalling these values. Format to currency and label the values **Total Values**.

7. Add a grand total in the report footer, label it **Overall Values** and format to currency.

8. Add controls to total the number of orders per **Make** and then add a grand total of number of orders in the report footer.

9. Name the controls holding the totals and use these names to calculate the percentage of orders for each **Make**. Label as **Percentage orders**.

10. Save and close the report and database.

18a – step 5

Order Details

Make	Price	Gadget	Number	Delivery
Brit publications				
	£25.00	Manual	3	01/01/2007
	£24.50	Manual	8	22/05/2006
	£24.50	Manual	3	16/05/2006
Average order			5	
Drakes				
	£12.35	Mouse	6	14/10/2006
Average order			6	
Pinco				
	£25.00	Mouse	3	14/09/2006
	£19.99	Mouse	8	23/05/2006
	£16.50	Mouse	6	14/04/2006
	£16.50	Mouse	1	02/03/2006
Average order			5	
Pritts				
	£199.00	Monitor	2	02/09/2006
	£9.99	Document holder	3	14/03/2006
Average order			3	
Stays				
	£336.99	Monitor	1	05/09/2006
	£19.99	Mouse	4	13/09/2006
Average order			3	
Treehouse books				
	£33.50	Manual	5	18/11/2006
	£18.50	Manual	2	18/09/2006
Average order			4	
Welstead				
	£205.00	Monitor	5	02/09/2006
	£157.99	Monitor	2	13/03/2006

18b – step 6

Order Details

Make	Price	Gadget	Number	Delivery
Brit publications				
	£25.00	Manual	3	01/01/2007
	£24.50	Manual	8	22/05/2006
	£24.50	Manual	3	16/05/2006
Total Values	£344.50			
Drakes				
	£12.35	Mouse	6	14/10/2006
Total Values	£74.10			

18c – step 9

	Document holder	1	12/05/2006

Total Values	£2,136.67		
Orders	31	*Percentage orders*	30.39%

Xana

	£199.00 Keyboard	1	08/06/2006
	£67.50 Keyboard	3	30/11/2006
	£33.50 Mouse	4	14/06/2006
	£24.50 Mouse	8	22/05/2006

Total Values	£731.50		
Orders	16	*Percentage orders*	15.69%

Overall Values	£4,686.61
Total orders	102

Exercise 19 1. Open the *Company* database.

2. Create a report based on the table displaying the following fields: Product Name, Category, Quantity per Unit, Unit Price, Units in stock and Units on order.

3. Save as *Products Report*.

4. Adjust columns so that all data is displayed.

5. Add controls to display the Stock Value for each Category: totals for Unit Price × Quantity in Stock.

6. Re-format the Unit Price and Stock Value controls to show the £ symbol.

7. Add a control in the report footer to display the Total Stock Value.

8. Finally, add a further control to show the Percentage value of stock for each category. Format values to two decimals.

9. Save and close the file.

19a – step 6 – Stock Value for Category 1

Products Report

Category	Product Name	Quantity Per Unit	Unit Price	Units In Stock	Units On Order
1					
	Chartreuse verte	750 cc per bottle	£18.00	69	0
	Chang	24 - 12 oz bottles	£19.00	17	40
	Guaraná Fantástica	12 - 355 ml cans	£4.50	20	0
	Sasquatch Ale	24 - 12 oz bottles	£14.00	111	0
	Steeleye Stout	24 - 12 oz bottles	£18.00	20	0
	Chai	10 boxes x 20 bags	£18.00	39	0
	Côte de Blaye	12 - 75 cl bottles	£263.50	17	0
	Ipoh Coffee	16 - 500 g tins	£46.00	17	10
	Laughing Lumberjack Lager	24 - 12 oz bottles	£14.00	52	0
	Rhönbräu Klosterbier	24 - 0.5 l bottles	£7.75	125	0
	Outback Lager	24 - 355 ml bottles	£15.00	15	10
	Lakkalikööri	500 ml	£18.00	57	0

Stock value   £12,480.25

19b – step 9 – final page of report

	Røgede sild	1k pkg.	£9.50	5	70
	Spegesild	4 - 450 g glasses	£12.00	95	0
	Escargots de Bourgogne	24 pieces	£13.25	62	0
	Inlagd Sill	24 - 250 g jars	£19.00	112	0

Stock value   £13,010.35   *Percentage*   17.55%

Total Stock Value   £74,140.85

EXERCISE 20

You will need to know how to:

- Create running summaries in a report
- Insert a data field into a report header/footer
- Force page breaks for groups in reports

1. Open the *Holiday* database.

2. Create a report based on the *Hotel* table that groups hotels by **Country**.

3. Create a running summary of the number of bedrooms for hotels in each country. Format the final total to show a separator.

4. Now force page breaks in the report so that hotels within each country are on a separate page.

5. Add a calculated control in the report footer (now page 4) to count up the number of hotels overall. Add the label: **Hotel number**.

6. Amend the label for the running summary to **total bedrooms**.

7. Save and close the report and database.

20a – step 3

Hotel Details

Country	Name	Bedrooms	Swimming Pool	Miles from airport
Cyprus				
	Coral	24	☐	75
	Serino	55	☐	65
Sum		79		
France				
	Grande	35	☑	87
	Madagasca	43	☐	26
	San Moreno	150	☑	50
Sum		307		
Italy				
	Giorgio	200	☑	30
Sum		507		
Spain				
	Granada	186	☑	12
	Hiltonian	200	☑	20
	Turina	187	☑	33
Sum		1,080		

20b – step 6

Country	Name	Bedrooms	Swimming Pool	Miles from airport
Spain				
	Granada	186	☑	12
	Hiltonian	200	☑	20
	Turina	187	☑	33
total bedrooms		*1,080*		
Hotel number:		9		

EXERCISE 21

You will need to know how to:

◗ Link external data to a database

◗ Record a simple macro

◗ Run a macro

◗ Assign a macro to a control, form or report

AM5.6.1 & AM5.5.1

1. Open the *Orders* database.

2. Link it to the spreadsheet *Gadgets* and save the new table as *Gadget details*.

3. Correct the spelling of **ergonomic** in the **keyboard** details.

4. Add the following colours for the manual: **black & white**, **greyscale**, **coloured**.

5. Save these changes and check that details in the spreadsheet have been updated.

6. Create a form based on all the fields in the *Contact details* table.

7. Record a macro that will go to a new record in the form. Name it **New Record**.

8. Attach it to the *Contact details* form as a button and check that it works.

9. Now create a command button on the *Order details* form and label it Gadget details.

10. Record and save a macro that will open the *Gadget details* table.

11. Assign the macro to the **Gadget details** command button.

12. Save and close the database.

21a – step 2

🗐	Create table in Design view
🗐	Create table by using wizard
🗐	Create table by entering data
▦	Contact details
◄▨	Gadget details
▦	Manuals and document holders
▦	Order Details

21b – step 7

Action	Comment
▶ GoToRecord	Goes to first new record

New Record : Macro

Action Arguments

Object Type	Form
Object Name	Contact details
Record	New
Offset	

Makes the specified record the current record in a table, form, or query result set. Press F1 for help on this action.

21c – step 8

21d – step 11

EXERCISES 22 AND 23

You will need to know how to:

▶ Show duplicates in queries

▶ Show unmatched values in queries

Exercise 22 1. Open the *Activities* database and add the following two records to the *Members* table:

GX778	Hans	WR3	Yr2A
PT442	Meryl	WR3	Learning Support

2. Create a query named *Club members* that will display the names of all the clubs, the names of the members and their classes.

3. Now create a find duplicates query based on *Club members* that will check for duplicate values in the **Club** field: display just the name of the club and numbers of members.

4. Save the query as *Most Popular Clubs*.

5. Design a new query that will find all the clubs that have no members. Display the fields: **Code**, **Club**, **Day** and **Location** and save as **Clubs Without Members**.

22a – step 2

Club members : Select Query		
Club	**Name**	**Class**
Chess for all	Tim	Yr2A
Computing for all	Mary	Yr3B
Warhammer	Roy	Yr1B
Chess for all	Harry	Learning Support
Indian cookery	Ali	Yr3B
Indian cookery	Kathy	Yr1B
Writing	Lorna	Yr2A
Writing	Hans	Yr2A
Writing	Meryl	Learning Support

22b – step 4

Most Popular Clubs : Sel...	
Club Field	**NumberOfDups**
Chess for all	2
Indian cookery	2
▶ Writing	3

Record: |◀|◀| 3 |▶|▶|▶*|

22c

Code	Club	Day	Location
CH1	Chess for beginners	Wednesday	C4
DR4	Drama	Wednesday	Hall
SQ2	Squash	Monday	Sports hall
CO4	Computing for beginners	Monday	C4
CO6	Cookery	Tuesday	Kitchen

Clubs Without Members : Select Query

Record: 1 of 5

Exercise 23 1. Open the *Company* database.

2. Create a query to find all records with a Reorder Level that is not 0. Display the **Product Name**, **Category**, **Unit Price** and **Reorder Level**.

3. Save as *Positive Reorder Level*.

4. Create a query based on the *Positive Reorder Level* query to display the numbers of all duplicated order levels.

5. Now search for all records that are not **Discontinued** and are not in **Categories 3–8**. Display only **Product Name** and **Category**.

6. Save as *Current Low Categories*.

7. Close the file.

23a – step 4

ReorderLevel Field	NumberOfDups
5	8
10	7
15	10
20	9
25	12
30	8

23b – step 5

Product Name	Category
Chai	1
Chang	1
Aniseed Syrup	2
Chef Anton's Cajun Seasoning	2
Grandma's Boysenberry Spread	2
Northwoods Cranberry Sauce	2
Genen Shouyu	2
Sasquatch Ale	1
Steeleye Stout	1
Côte de Blaye	1
Chartreuse verte	1
Ipoh Coffee	1
Gula Malacca	2
Sirop d'érable	2
Vegie-spread	2
Louisiana Fiery Hot Pepper Sauce	2
Louisiana Hot Spiced Okra	2
Laughing Lumberjack Lager	1
Outback Lager	1
Rhönbräu Klosterbier	1
Lakkalikööri	1
Original Frankfurter grüne Soße	2

You will need to know how to:

▶ Create and edit a one-to-one relationship between tables

▶ Apply inner and outer joins

▶ Show highest, lowest range of values in queries

〈ECDL〉 **AM5.1.2**

1. Open the *Records* database.

2. Assign the primary key to the appropriate field in the *managers* table so that you can create a one-to-one relationship with the *label* table.

3. Link the two tables.

4. Edit the relationship to enforce referential integrity.

5. Link the *label* and *bands* tables using the **LabelID** field.

6. Now edit the link to enforce referential integrity and create a one-to-many relationship.

7. Link the *bands* and *stock* tables using the **BandID** field.

8. You want to set up a query to find all the records in stock. As you have some stock where there are no details in the *bands* table, edit the join so that you will see all your stock. Display the following fields only: **Band name, Style, Number in stock, Album Title.**

9. Save the query as *Records in stock*.

10. Now edit the join again to show only stock where you have details of the bands.

11. Finally, create a query that will display the top five best-selling titles in the charts. Display just the **Song title** and **Number bought.**

12. Save as *Top 5* and then close the query.

24a – step 3

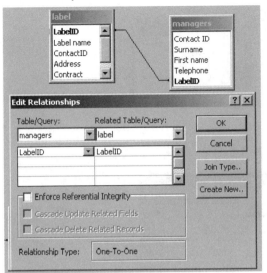

24b – step 5

24c – step 9

Band name	Style	Number in stock	Album Title
Out of the blue	Rock	10	Best songs
Black is black	Soul	5	Top sellers
Skyward	Blues	25	Best of the bunch
The two men	Blues	7	Play our song
Happy Daze	Rock	15	Music to swing to
Kerumph	Classical	12	All the rage
Manhattan	Soul	19	In luck
Artisan	Classical	5	Psychadelica
Make up your n	Heavy metal	28	Sorted
Razzmatazz	Soul	16	Evening love songs
Stoney	Heavy metal	3	Weather map
Weightless	Rock	2	Go now
Out of the blue	Rock	14	20 best hits
The two men	Blues	7	Greatest from the two men
Artisan	Classical	16	School is over
		9	Where are you?
Happy Daze	Rock	12	Get it now
		25	Top hits
		18	Will you dance?

24d – step 10 – edited join

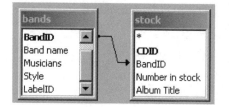

24e – step 11

Query1 : Select Query	
Song title	Number bought
Hello goodbye	6550
Stay with me	5990
Yes	5668
Mozart Choral	4508
When will I see you	4224

EXERCISE 25

You will need to know how to:

▶ Apply self joins in queries

〈ECDL〉 **AM5.1.2**

1. In the *Records* database you want to find out if any bands share the same record label.

2. Create a query based on two *bands* tables, displaying just the BandID, Band name and LabelID.

3. Set the query properties so that there are no duplicate records displayed.

4. Sort the LabelID field alphabetically.

5. Save as *shared label*.

6. Close the database.

25a

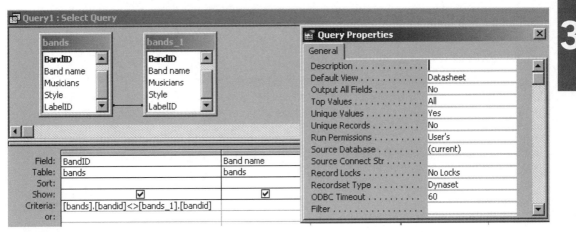

BandID	Band name	LabelID
BB2	Black is black	D335
MN4	Manhattan	D335
RZ4	Razzmatazz	D335
AR5	Artisan	H886
KR3	Kerumph	H886
MU2	Make up your mind	R227
ST6	Stoney	R227
OB4	Out of the blue	V556
SK7	Skyward	V556
WT7	Weightless	V556

25b – query design

PART 4

Module AM6: Presentation, Advanced Level

To pass this module, you must be able to appreciate the role of various aspects of a presentation; link files; import and edit pictures and other objects; use sounds, videos and animations; create appropriate charts; manage slide shows and use automated features such as macros.

You will need to understand the importance of:

▸ Numbers of people and the room environment

▸ Different types of audience

▸ Choice of images, texts and colours

▸ Timing

⟨ECDL⟩ **AM6.1.1 & AM6.1.2**

Q1: With a large audience, what fonts work better on slide images?
1a. serif
1b. sans serif

Q2: What is a sensible number of slides per minute?
2a. no more than 1
2b. 2–3
2c. 4–5
2d. it doesn't matter

Q3: If you prefer dark backgrounds, which colour would you choose for the whole presentation?
3a. blue
3b. red
3c. black
3d. a range of colours

Q4: A presentation prepared for parents must now be shown to 14-year olds. What is the one change you would make?
4a. add cartoons and animations
4b. cut down on the text
4c. re-think the whole presentation
4d. no change

Q5: Ideally, what is the maximum number of lines per slide?
5a. 12
5b. 8–10
5c. 4–6
5d. 3

Q1 – 1b. From the back of a hall, simpler text is easier to read against an image or on a chart.

Q2 – 2b. Waiting a full minute for each slide could become boring. However, changing slides more rapidly than once every 20–30 seconds will not allow enough time for the audience to take in the contents.

Q3 – 3a. Blue is easier on the eye than black and red should be kept for impact and to highlight text or objects on slides. Changing colours will lose consistency.

Q4 – 4c. Presentations should always be planned with the audience in mind. An adult audience may well have greater knowledge or different needs to a group of teenagers. It may therefore require a drastic reworking of the whole presentation, rather than changing elements on individual slides.

Q5 – 5c. Too many lines of text will be hard to read and the key points will be difficult to absorb or remember.

EXERCISE 6

You will need to know how to:

- Merge a Word outline into a presentation
- Apply different fill effects to the background

 AM6.2.1

1. Export the Word document *Sleep* to PowerPoint and save as *Sleeping.ppt*.

2. Apply a 2-colour gradient fill effect. Use white and orange and select a *diagonal down* style. Apply to all the slides.

3. On Slide 5 only, titled **Drugs**, change the background to any patterned fill effect in orange and white.

4. Change the first point on this slide to read: **Use 3 nights maximum.**

5. Save and close the file.

6

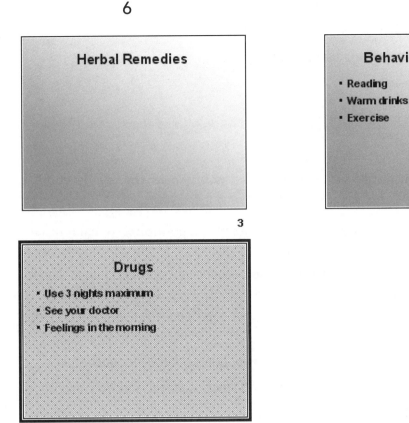

EXERCISE 7

You will need to know how to:

▶ Create and save a presentation template

▶ Merge presentations

▶ Save a slide as an image

◁ECDL▷ **AM6.2.1 & AM6.2.2**

1. Start a new presentation and create a template as follows:

   a. Title font: Arial Black 42.

   b. Level 1 font: Arial Black 30, italic with black circular bullets.

   c. Level 2 font: Arial 28, indented with square bullets.

   d. Background: gradient effect mixing green and white.

2. Save as *Insomnia* and use for the following presentation.

3. Create a slide titled Herbal Remedies.

4. Add the following text as bullet points:

   Chamomile Tea
   Nutmeg
   Valerian Root
   Passionflower
   Hops

5. After Chamomile Tea, add the words: Most popular choice at level 2.

6. Save the presentation.

7. Now insert the image *chamomile*. Resize and position it so that it fills the right-hand side of the slide.

8. Save this slide as a jpg image somewhere on your computer. Name it *herbal*.

9. Insert all the slides from *Sleeping* except Slide 3 into the presentation *Insomnia*.

10. Move your current Herbal Remedies slide so that it becomes Slide 3.

11. Finally, locate the image *herbal* and check that it has saved correctly.

12. Close all open files.

7a – step 5

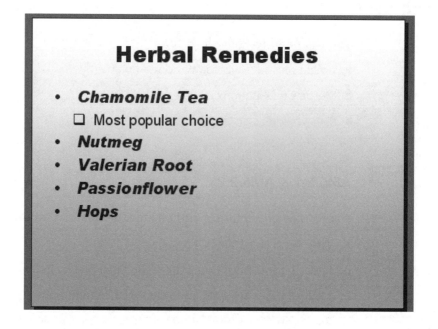

7b – step 10

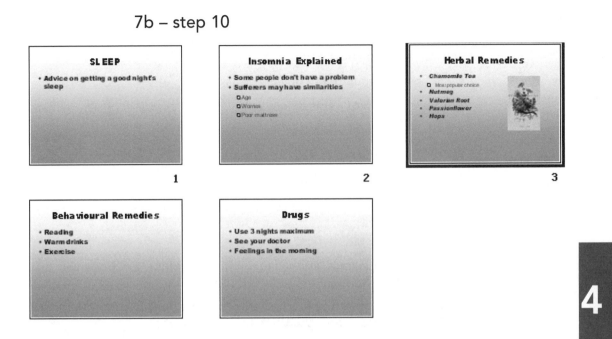

7c – step 11

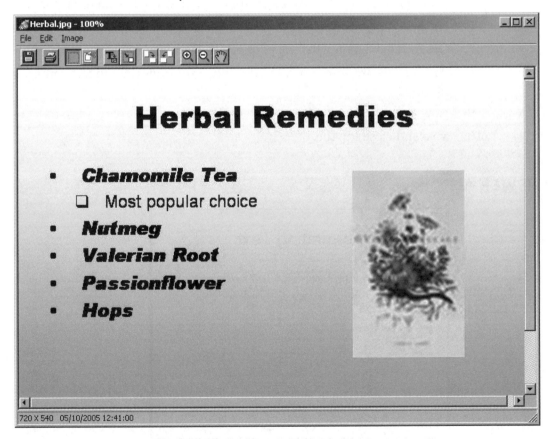

4

You will need to know how to:

- Group or ungroup drawn objects
- Bring objects backwards or forwards
- Distribute objects using specified co-ordinates
- Position objects horizontally or vertically

〈ECDL〉 **AM6.3.1**

Exercise 8
1. Open the presentation *Text*.
2. Ungroup the diagram and change the fill colour for Underline and Shadow to pale orange.
3. Move the arrow pointing to the shadow toolbar button further to the left so that it is more clearly positioned on the button.
4. Regroup the diagram and reduce it in size.
5. Draw an ellipse that is just larger than the diagram and fill it with green.
6. Position it behind the diagram.
7. Group the diagram with the ellipse.
8. Position the grouped drawing vertically 5 cm from the top left corner of the slide.
9. Now align it horizontally relative to the slide.
10. Save and close the file.

ANSWER 8

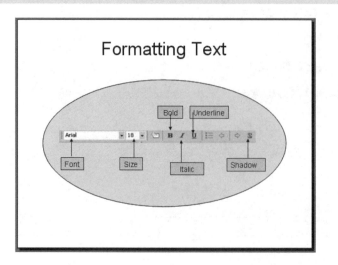

Exercise 9 1. Start a new presentation and select a blank slide layout.

2. Create an AutoShape star that is 8 cm high and apply a yellow fill.

3. Copy it three times and position a shape in each corner of the slide.

4. Draw a large rectangle to fill most of the slide. Apply an orange fill and send it behind the stars.

5. Align two stars at the top relative to the slide, and two at the bottom.

6. Now make sure that the two left-hand stars are horizontally 1 cm from the top left-hand corner; and the two right-hand stars are horizontally 14 cm from the top left-hand corner.

7. Create a different style of star, colour it red and position it in the centre of the slide.

8. Align this star vertically and horizontally.

9. Check that it is centrally positioned by displaying guidelines.

10. Group all the shapes and reduce the grouped shape in size.

11. Position it in the bottom right-hand corner of the slide.

12. Save as *Stars* and then close the file.

9a – step 7

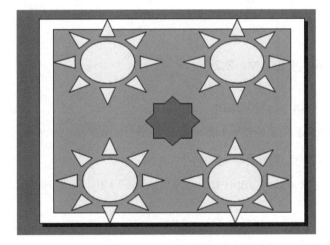

9b

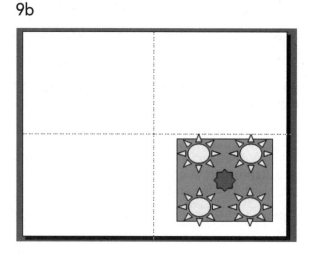

EXERCISE 10

You will need to know how to:

- Omit background graphics from a slide
- Apply a semi-transparent effect to an object
- Apply 3-D effects to an object
- Apply and reposition a coloured shadow.

◊ECDL◊ **AM6.3.1 & AM6.3.2**

1. Open the presentation *Tennis*.
2. Go to Slide 4 and remove the background graphics on this slide only.
3. Insert the image *sandwiches*.
4. Add the following text to this slide as a list: Bar, Restaurant and Reading Room.
5. Increase the size of the image and apply a red-coloured shadow to the bottom right-hand corner.
6. On Slide 5, add the text: St. Worthington Cup.
7. Add a ribbon auto shape and apply a fill colour and semi-transparent effect.
8. Increase the size of the image. Position it across part of the text, making sure the words are still visible.

9. Add the following text lower down the slide: Valentine Tournament.

10. Insert a heart-shaped auto shape, colour it red and apply a 3-D effect.

11. Return to Slide 4 and reposition the shadow so that it is across the top left-hand corner.

12. Save the updated presentation and close the file.

10a – step 5

10b – step 10

You will need to know how to:

- Change the colour depth of an image
- Crop and rescale an image
- Rotate, flip or mirror an image
- Convert an image into greyscale or black & white

AM6.3.3

1. Open the file *Jungle*.

2. On Slide 2, crop the Lion image to remove the wall.

3. Increase the size of the leopard image in proportion to match the height of the lion image exactly and flip it horizontally so that it faces inwards.

4. Change the leopard image to greyscale.

5. Add the labels **LION** and **LEOPARD** under the images.

6. On Slide 4, move the picture to make way for an exact copy.

7. Copy the picture into an appropriate programme and decrease the colour depth. Then copy this new image onto the slide.

8. Flip one of the images horizontally to face in the opposite direction.

9. Save the file.

11a – step 5

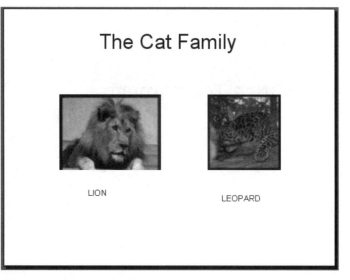

11b

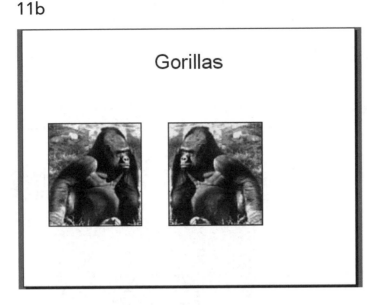

You will need to know how to:

▶ Convert an image into a different file type

▶ Apply special effects

▶ Apply fill effects to a drawn object

▶ Apply a style from one object to another

 AM6.3.2 & AM6.3.3

Exercise 12 1. Open the image *snake charmer* with a suitable program and apply a paint effect such as *brush strokes*.

2. Insert this image into the top right-hand corner of Slide 3 of *Jungle*. Increase the size so that it is clearly visible.

3. Save the image as a GIF file with the name *snake charmer2*.

4. On Slide 3, draw a trapezoid Autoshape to look like a basket and add a woven textured fill effect.

5. Apply a 3-D effect.

6. Draw a rectangle shape in the top left-hand corner and apply the style used for the basket.

7. Save and close the file.

ANSWER 12

Exercise 13 1. Start a new presentation and on Slide 1 add the title **Strange Birds**.

2. Open *Puffin.jpg*.

3. Save it as a GIF file.

4. Apply a special effect, e.g. page curl.

5. Add the image to your slide.

6. Create an oval shape and send it behind the objects on the slide.

7. Add a thick border and textured fill effect, e.g. water droplets.

8. Draw a small irregular shape, e.g. an explosion AutoShape, in one corner of the slide and apply the style of the oval shape.

9. Save as *Strange Birds* and then close the presentation.

13

Strange Birds

You will need to know how to:

 Change chart type

 Create a mixed chart

 Change Y-axis scale

 Change chart type for a data series

 Display different Y-axis units

◊ECDL◊ **AM6.4.1**

1. Open the presentation *Department Store*.

2. On Slide 2, change the chart to a line-column on two axes chart where Increase/Decrease in sales is shown as a line.

3. Add titles to the axes: Linen Sets, Numbers Sold and Change in Sales.

4. Reformat the line so that it is clearly visible.

5. Change the scale of the Y-axis so that it shows the range 15–75 and set the maximum unit at 5.

6. Display the numbers of sets sold in hundreds.

7. Finally, change the display of the 2003 sales to an area style.

8. Save and close the presentation.

14a – step 4

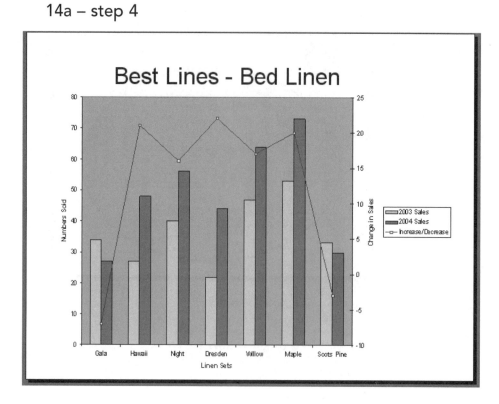

14b

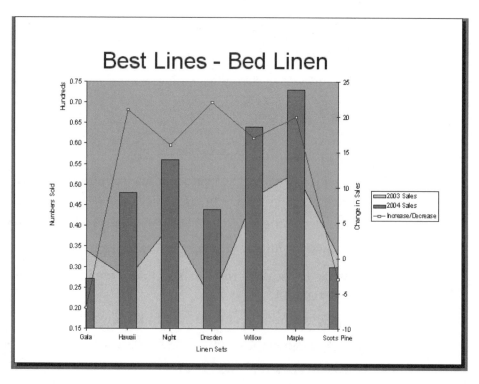

You will need to know how to:

▶ Draw a flowchart

▶ Change or delete flowchart shapes

▶ Change connectors

⟨ECDL⟩ **AM6.4.2**

1. Open the presentation *Cooking*.

2. On Slide 1, add a connector between Salted? and Soak overnight.

3. Change the Carve and eat shape to a rectangle.

4. Make sure the text Leave covered several hours fits within the shape.

5. Change the first connector from Start so that it does not display an arrow.

6. Remove the Heat oven shape completely; amend the connectors so there is no obvious gap.

7. Adjust any connectors or labels to improve the appearance of the flowchart and add a patterned fill effect to the shapes.

8. On Slide 2, create the following flowchart using appropriate shapes and connectors:

   Start – Buy seeds – Decide numbers for your plot – Plant, weed and water – Harvest – End

9. Add a diamond shape between Decide numbers and Plant, weed and water. Enter the text: Hard shell? Link this to a rectangle containing the text: Soak overnight and add Yes and No labels.

10. Add a gradient fill to the shapes.

11. Save and close the presentation.

15a – step 7

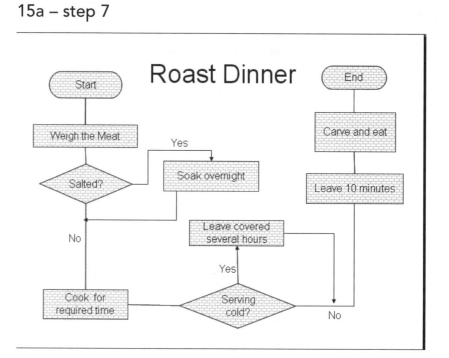

15b

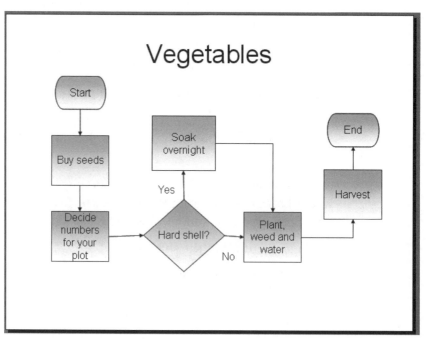

EXERCISE 16

You will need to know how to:

▶ Insert sounds into a presentation

▶ Insert movies into a presentation

AM6.5.1

1. Open the presentation *Jungle*.

2. Insert the image *explorer* into Slide 1 and apply an entry effect, e.g. box.

3. Add the sound *Tiger* to play automatically when the slide appears.

4. Add the movie *catlick2* to Slide 4, apply an entry animation effect and set the animation to play automatically.

5. Save and close the file.

ANSWER 16

EXERCISES 17 AND 18

You will need to know how to:

▶ Animate objects

▶ Change the sequence of animation

▶ Apply a dimming animation effect

Exercise 17 1. Open the presentation *Insomnia*.

2. On Slide 3, apply an entrance custom animation effect to the list items, e.g. fly in from the bottom.

3. Make the list dim to green.

4. If you can, make the level 2 entry (**Most popular choice**) dim to a different colour, e.g. blue.

5. Apply the following custom effect to the title: grow/shrink.

6. Run the slide show.

7. Now change the sequence so that the title is animated before the list items appear.

8. On Slide 4, add a final list item: Soothing bath.

9. Insert the image *bath* and apply an exit custom animation, e.g. fade, that will apply automatically without a mouse click. Add a suitable sound effect.

10. Save and close the presentation.

17a – step 4

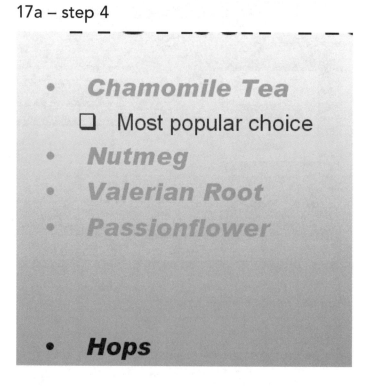

17b – step 7

Exercise 18 1. Open *Strange Birds*.

2. Apply a shrink/grow animation to the picture.

3. Apply an entrance animation, e.g. fly in, to the title text.

4. Apply an exit animation to the explosion shape, e.g. wheel.

5. Run the slide show to check the animations.

6. Now change the sequence so the text is animated first.

7. Dim the text to blue after animation.

8. Save these changes and close the presentation.

18a – step 4

18b

EXERCISES 19 AND 20

You will need to know how to:

- Animate chart elements
- Set up navigation links and buttons
- Reroute navigation aides

 AM6.5.2 & AM6.6.1

Exercise 19 1. Open the presentation *Insomnia*.

2. Create a new Slide 4 with the title Weight.

3. Add a 2-D column chart using the figures set out below:

Categories	Males 2001	Females 2001
Underweight	4	6
Desirable	28	38
Overweight	47	33
Obese	21	23

4. Give the chart the title: Body Mass Index.

5. Label the X-axis **Categories** and the Y-axis **Numbers**.

6. Format the data series in different shades of green.

7. Now apply an entry custom animation that will dissolve in the male data series automatically and then the female data series on a mouse click.

8. On Slide 2, add an extra list item: **Overweight**.

9. Use this text as a navigation link to Slide 5.

10. On Slide 3, add an action button that will link to the website www.naturopathy.org.uk.

11. Edit the link on Slide 2 so that it navigates to Slide 4, not 5.

12. Save the presentation.

19a – step 7

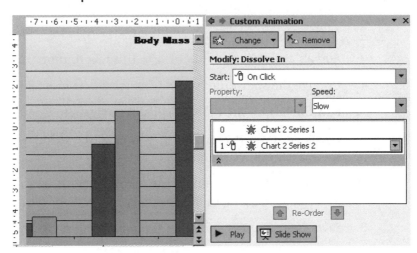

19b – step 10

19c – step 11

Edit Hyperlink

Link to:

Text to display: Overweight

ScreenTip...

Existing File or Web Page

Place in This Document

Create New Document

E-mail Address

Select a place in this document:

- First Slide
- Last Slide
- Next Slide
- Previous Slide
- Slide Titles
  - 1. SLEEP
  - 2. Insomnia Explained
  - 3. Herbal Remedies
  - 4. Weight
  - 5. Behavioural Remedies
  - 6. Drugs
- Custom Shows

Slide preview:

Weight

☐ Show and return

Remove Link

OK   Cancel

Exercise 20 1. Open the presentation *Company Contributions*.

2. At the bottom of Slide 2, add the text: Organiser – Mary Aspel.

3. Add an action button link next to this text to move to Contacts – Slide 4.

4. Change the slide order so that Contacts becomes Slide 3.

5. Edit the link so the button will still navigate to Contacts.

6. Use the text: Charity on Slide 4 as a link to the website www.savethechildren.org.uk.

7. On the same slide, animate the chart elements by category so that data for each year dissolves in separately.

8. Save these changes and close the presentation.

20a – step 3

20b – step 5

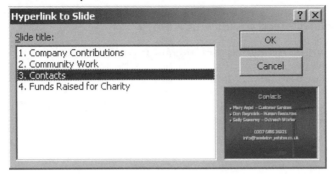

20c – step 6

20d

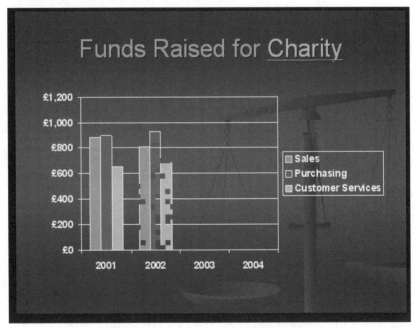

You will need to know how to:

▶ Apply/remove transition timings

▶ Loop a presentation

▶ Change settings to present the slide show with or without animations or automatic timings

 AM6.6.1

1. In the presentation *Insomnia*, apply a slow fade transition to all the slides.

2. Set the timing to advance the slides automatically after five seconds.

3. Select Slide 4 and change the transition on this slide only to a slow dissolve that advances with a mouse click.

4. Set the show to loop continuously and then run it.

5. Now change the settings: advance the slides manually, do not loop and do not show animations.

6. Save and close the presentation.

21a – step 2

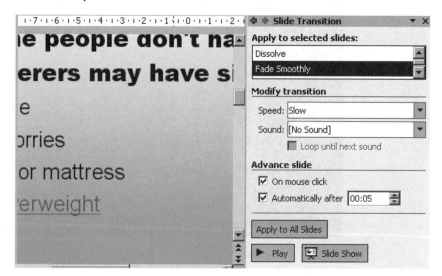

21b – step 5

Set Up Show

Show type
- ● Presented by a speaker (full screen)
- ○ Browsed by an individual (window)
  - ☐ Show scrollbar
- ○ Browsed at a kiosk (full screen)

Show slides
- ● All
- ○ From: [ ] To: [ ]
- ○ Custom show:
  - [ ]

Show options
- ☐ Loop continuously until 'Esc'
- ☐ Show without narration
- ☑ Show without animation

Pen color: [ ] ▼

Advance slides
- ● Manually
- ○ Using timings, if present

Multiple monitors
Display slide show on:
[Primary Monitor] ▼
- ☐ Show Presenter View

Performance
- ☐ Use hardware graphics acceleration   [Tips]

Slide show resolution: [Use Current Resolution] ▼

[OK]   [Cancel]

EXERCISE 22

You will need to know how to:

▶ Create a custom slide show

▶ Run the slide show

▶ Edit the slide show

‹ECDL›   **AM6.6.2**

1. Open the presentation *Tennis*.

2. Apply a transition, e.g. vertical blinds, to all the slides.

3. Create a custom slide show named *Playing Tennis* that includes Slides 1, 2, 5 & 6 in that order.

4. Run the show.

5. Now edit it as follows:

   a. Add Facilities as Slide 5.

   b. Re-order the slides so that Location is now Slide 5.

6. Run the show again.

7. Save the presentation.

22 – step 5b

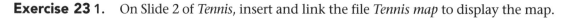

Define Custom Show [?][X]

Slide show name: Playing Tennis

Slides in presentation:
1. St. Worthington
2. Location
3. Membership
4. Facilities
5. Events
6. Open Evening

[Add >>]
[Remove]

Slides in custom show:
1. St. Worthington
2. Events
3. Open Evening
4. Facilities
5. Location

[↑]
[↓]

[OK] [Cancel]

EXERCISES 23 AND 24

▶ Link the contents of separate files, e.g. text or charts

▶ Update and modify links

▶ Change a linked object to an embedded object

▶ Insert and link an image

 AM6.7.1

Exercise 23 1. On Slide 2 of *Tennis*, insert and link the file *Tennis map* to display the map.

2. Open the document and add the words in red underneath the caption.

3. Back on the slide, update the link.

4. On Slide 3, insert the chart from the file *Club membership* as a linked object.

5. Open the spreadsheet file, change **Guests** in 2004 to 35 and update the chart on the slide.

6. Now change the chart to an embedded object.

7. Finally, insert the image *invitation* and make sure it is linked to the file.

8. Enlarge the image in size and add the following text across the centre: 25 June from 4.00 – 8.00 pm.

9. Save and close the presentation.

10. (If you can, open the image *Invitation* into an editing programme, add some text, e.g. **Welcome**, across the top and then save the file. Now re-open your presentation and update the links. You should see your text appear on the image.)

23a – step 3

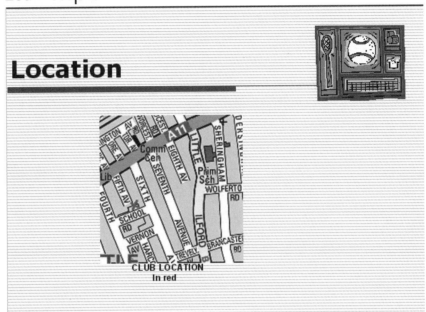

23b – step 5

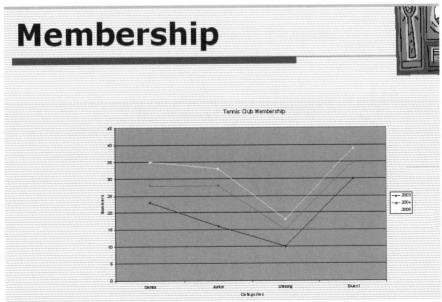

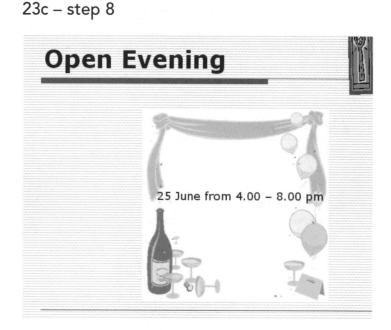

Exercise 24 1. Open *Company Contributions*.

2. Insert and link the image *logo* and position it centrally at the top of Slide 1.

3. If you can, open the image in an editing package and make changes, e.g. using artistic effects. Save with the same name.

4. Return to the slide and update the linked image.

5. On Slide 4, delete the chart and insert the linked chart from the file *Company data*.

6. Open the spreadsheet file and make the following changes: in 2003, sales raised £950 and purchasing £1,400. Customer services raised £875 in 2004.

7. Update the linked chart.

8. Change it to an embedded chart.

9. On the original chart, change the amount raised by sales in 2001 to £400 and try to update the chart on the slide.

10. Save and close all files.

24a – step 4

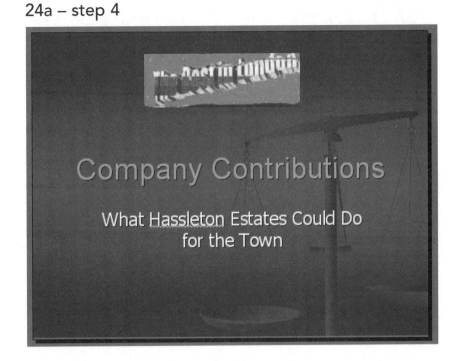

24b – step 7

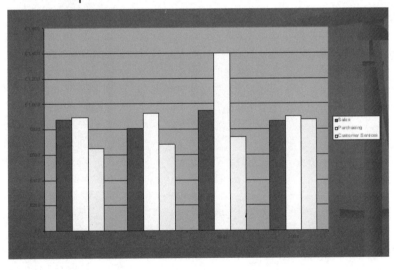

EXERCISE 25

You will need to know how to:

- Record a macro
- Run a macro
- Assign a macro to a custom button on the toolbar

1. Open the *Tennis* presentation.

2. Record a macro that will highlight the map on Slide 2 when the mouse is over the image.

3. Run the slide show and check that the macro works.

4. Assign the macro to a custom button on the toolbar.

5. Apply the macro to the heart image on Slide 5 and check that it works.

6. Save and close the presentation.

25 – step 4

Licensing Agreement

This book comes with a CD. By opening this package, you are agreeing to be bound by the following: